MARK DANDO is an author, a mentor, c [barcode: I0067483]
a poet.

He works with a small team of highly talented developers: Doug Richardson, Alison Rogers, Andrew Manuel and Luke Thomas.

He co-founded what became Coloured Square Limited with Doug in 2000. Together their provocative and powerful "structured common-sense" system of learning and development continues to receive rave reviews from individuals and organisations who want help to improve their management, leadership, sales, influence, presenting – in short anything which requires more skill in communication. Their favourite brief is to help organisations change their approach to the business of learning and development itself – improving speed to competence and engagement.

Mark has been an author since 2013. This is his fourth book written for people who want to change their thinking and improve their skills. His first three books are about attitudes to time, attitudes to presenting and the attitudes and activities required to improve personal well-being. He has published two children's books: *The Boy Who Yawned*, and *The Boy Who Kidnapped Father Christmas*. A third children's book (*with a girl in the title*) is finished and ready to go.

Starting in 2019, he's been putting some of his energy into poetry. He can be seen and heard performing at spoken word events in Bristol and Bath on a regular basis.

When he's not writing, developing people, or performing poetry, he plays the guitar, practises Tai Chi, tries to beat his children at table tennis, and plays games of all kinds.

He lives in Bristol with his wife and children.

To find out more visit the Coloured Square website at www.colouredsquare.com

Also by Mark Dando

Don't Strain LittleBrain

Also by Mark Dando and Doug Richardson

Squeeze Your Time
Kill the Robot

Children's books by Mark Dando

The Boy Who Yawned
The Boy Who Kidnapped Father Christmas

Coach-Sell-Teach-Tell™

A Mindset Book

Mark Dando with Doug Richardson

SilverWood

Published in 2020 by SilverWood Books

SilverWood Books Ltd
14 Small Street, Bristol, BS1 1DE, United Kingdom
www.silverwoodbooks.co.uk

Copyright © Mark Dando 2020
Images and Illustrations © Mark Dando 2020
Coach-Sell-Teach-Tell™ © Coloured Square Limited 2020
Used with permission.

The right of Mark Dando to be identified as the author
of this work has been asserted in accordance with the Copyright,
Designs and Patents Act 1988 Sections 77 and 78.

ISBN 978-1-78132-961-0 (paperback)
ISBN 978-1-78132-962-7 (ebook)

British Library Cataloguing in Publication Data
A CIP catalogue record for this book is available from the British Library

Page design and typesetting by SilverWood Books

Contents

Introduction

We still need a revolution in how we develop people at work. It's so seldom any good. Too often, all that's provided by managers and developers is a guided tour of how to do the tasks required: how to push the right buttons, in the right order; how to fill in the correct forms; how to check the standards of the operation; how to say the correct phrases ("Sorry to keep you waiting", "Have a nice day!").

All this is vital for an individual's success in the job concerned and it needs to continue. But as soon as someone demonstrates they can fulfil the basics of their job, it reaches its limit. The development that managers and developers provide still so rarely goes beyond this – it still rarely actually develops *the quality of the person* involved.

The problem is, once they've learned the basics, it's always the *quality of the person* involved that finally affects their ability to become good at the job.

Increasingly, I believe that, once the person has got the button-pushing basics, the list of qualities that affect whether or not they become good at a job is small. In no particular order, it's things like the ability to:

- Make information interesting for others.
- Establish and maintain rapport.
- Communicate clearly and succinctly.
- Think things through in a structured manner.

- Be assertive.
- Manage themselves – their response to people and situations.
- Break rapport consciously when appropriate.
- Organise themselves and their work.
- Make decisions.
- Manage their own energy, focus, and effort.
- Manage the balance of attention they put into activities inside and outside work, which will keep them in a good *productive* state, and keep them out of unproductive or harmful levels of stress.

These are the kinds of skills that really make the difference between someone who can do a job and someone who can do a job well. But, typically, we're expected to learn such skills 'through experience'. Given time, by ourselves, we will learn many of them – but rarely all, and not necessarily the ones that we as individuals actually need the most.

This doesn't make sense – if such skills are learned through experience, then an experienced manager will have them (well, at least one or two of them). So, they could pass them on to their team. Yet, they rarely do! We're keeping a lid on the capability level of our workforce and then wondering why we can't seem to hit our key service metrics, or why we can't seem to get a better score in the hideous organisational engagement survey!?

If you're lucky, your manager tells you to watch a TED Talk or sends you on a workshop – which gets you started, for sure. But going on a one-day Time Management course isn't the same as learning personal organisation. The majority of skills listed above need regular, continual development. They're projects for a lifetime. There are plenty of studies and learning theory available for us to be sure that workshops aren't where the lasting development takes place. It might begin there, of course, but the rest needs to happen via day-to-day, hour-by-hour implementation, practice, review, discussion, drawing conclusions, trying again.

Since so much learning happens between formal inputs, you either need to be a self-starter – relentlessly on your own case with your learning – or get yourself an element of meaningful supervision (someone else on your case). If this meaningful supervision is from someone who sees and hears you in action on a semi-regular basis, so much the better.

By now, of course, I hear you shouting your objections at the page:

> You idiot! I don't have the time to finish my own tasks, let alone develop my people

> I don't have the skills needed to do it – that's why I send them on workshops!

> Nobody ever helped me develop my skills, and I've done OK

> I can't get them to do tasks correctly – why would they take my direction on skills?

All perfectly understandable objections. If any of these are yours then this is the book for you. We'll explore these and other challenges throughout, and use them as the springboard to solutions: alternative ways of thinking that will allow you to achieve more development with your people – more powerful development.

This book is for you if you want to provide people with transformative development in how they need to think and behave, so that they can do a better job (whatever their job).

It's for you if you'd like to find a way to do it easily and using little time.

It will challenge you to pass on your experience in an effective, skilful manner (Sell-Teach-Tell).

And, when you don't have the necessary experience or skill in the area required, it will challenge you to provide effective development via Coach, so that the person in front of you can go *beyond* your own capability.

Chapter One

Mindsets

Throughout this book, I'll highlight mindsets that we might affect in ourselves to provide better development. These will often appear in the pink and blue text boxes that you can already see lurking around. When I do this, I'm highlighting a specific process your brain uses to filter for information.

Our senses take in a huge deluge of information every second, millions of bits of data flooding in via eyes, ears, nose, etc. The brain would be overwhelmed if it actively tried to process all this information, so it doesn't. Our brains actively make decisions about what information to process and what information to filter out of our attention. Our conscious minds process approximately 120 bits of data per second. Listening to one person talking requires that we process sixty bits (i.e. half of our attention capacity[1]).

So, the majority of data we receive every second is discarded – not processed by our conscious mind.

As a result, we often miss large changes to our visual field and we can fail to notice something that is right in front of our eyes – something that would be obvious to somebody else who knows it's there, knows where to look, or knows it's about to happen.

1   Daniel, J. Levitin, *The Organized Mind*, Viking, 2015, p7

Every time I highlight 'mindsets' I'm challenging you to notice the process by which you 'set' your mind to filter for information, i.e. the largely unconscious neurological process by which your brain decides which 120 bits of information to pay attention to and what information to filter out or discard.

It's still not clear what sets your mind in this way, but it's probably a long list of factors: your beliefs, how you were brought up, the time of day, what you did yesterday, your physical state, how much alcohol you drank last night, how much exercise you've taken recently, how awake you are, how tired you are, the amount of glucose left in your prefrontal cortex, etc. (*Check out work by Simons and Chabris[2], Daniel J Levitin[3], Carol Dweck[4] or Richard Wiseman[5] for more detail.*)

One of the ways in which your mindsets may manifest themselves is in little unconscious instructions, rules or directions you give yourself – little ways in which you tell yourself to look at things...

`one way` or `another`

This book will explore simple but significant possibilities for replacing how you look at things `one way` with how you could look at things `another` in order to allow you to notice different information, select different behaviours, and make use of a more productive and efficient approach to the development of your people.

2 Daniel J Simons & Christopher Chabris, 'Gorillas in our midst: sustained inattentional blindness for dynamic events.' *Perception*, vol 28, 1999, pp1059-1074 (https://journals.sagepub.com/doi/abs/10.1068/p281059)
3 Daniel J. Levitin, *The Organized Mind*, Viking, 2015
4 Carol Dweck, *Mindset*, Robinson, 2012
5 Richard Wiseman, *Did You Spot The Gorilla*, Arrow, 2004

Chapter Two

Primary barriers

While there'll be a lot of little, functional mindset choices that will crop up as we go, there are several major issues, which are the basis for everything else. These primary ways of thinking (mindsets) or objections seem to prevent developers, coaches, managers and teachers from developing people efficiently and successfully. They're so prevalent – they crop up so regularly – that they've become myths, which many of us believe. This book sets out to address each of them in various ways.

Time

The **Development takes too much time – I don't have time to do it properly** myth.

We'll explore how to move from this to:

Keep it simple – keep it short and fast (then I can do more of it)

There'll be a chapter on time issues very shortly, but it's so significant that I'll reference it regularly until you're bored of it.

Skill

The **I must know what I'm doing** myth.

I don't – so I won't develop people

I'll send them on a workshop

This one's tempting. If you've had success and risen to your current lofty height of management or development by being good at technical, procedural tasks, then you may believe that behavioural skills are outside your remit. You may never have thought about them. As a result, you may have no idea what to do to develop them in people. So you don't! You pester others, asking for a workshop to develop them instead. *If this is you, then I hope by the end of this book you'll feel much more capable of identifying and working with people to develop these important skills – I hope you'll feel much more relaxed that you are capable enough to develop people in them.*

The second half of the book is intended to deal with key skills and disciplines you need to develop in yourself, so that you can improve your ability quickly. These skills are Rapport (connecting), Listening, Observing, Inhibiting (i.e. stopping your own immediate responses) and the discipline to stick with the simplicity of the four approaches – which will also be described in detail in the second half.

Lack of intention

Many developers and managers I've worked with over the last 20 years just aren't intending to change how the person is. This issue can be caused by many interlocking mindsets, but possibly the biggest culprit is the Soft Skills myth. This myth pretends that we can afford to relegate to an afterthought the interpersonal communication skills that are vital to success in most walks of life.

Nonsense.

Communication and personal effectiveness skills are hard – they're edgy; they're the cutting-through skills. If, when you do them, they're 'soft skills', then maybe you're doing them wrong.

Powerful, helpful listening isn't necessarily 'soft'; it can be hard as steel, sharp as a surgical instrument. Rapport isn't 'soft'; it can be as dynamic and powerful as a martial art. And these skills aren't easy either – they're difficult. If you're not a natural with them, then they can take considerable time and effort to develop properly. This last point means it's really important to:

Start developing them as soon as possible

I can't afford to wait 'til all the task stuff is correctly in place

So, as you read this book, I invite you to stop belittling and dismissing these skills as 'soft'. Instead, let's own up that we're not as skilled as we could be and put in the work that's needed to get to grips with them. We'll explore how to move to:

I must begin developing people in them immediately and quickly

Just have a go   and

If I help them with their skills, I can speed up their progress with the job greatly

Not even looking: lack of attention

Due to the lack of *intention*, many developers and managers I've worked with just aren't looking at the person and considering how they need to change. This can be caused by several of the above mindsets, or it may just be that the developer or manager is asleep at the wheel. In any case, we're going to be moving to a mindset of:

Let me get curious about what's *really* limiting their performance   and   It won't take much observation to identify what I should help develop in this person

We'll deal with this issue in several chapters about observation: how to observe enough (in several very short sessions) in order to spot the need; how to isolate a small enough chunk of information to address (so that it actually lands); and how to continue to observe to make decisions about which approach is best: Coach-Sell-Teach or Tell.

Autopilot

I have my approach – it's what I always do

This major mindset-barrier is powered by a number of regular and recurrent thinking patterns, which often crop up together. In my experience, these are really troublesome myths that get in the way of sensible, practical development: I should Coach everything. Coaching is best because it creates buy-in. Teaching is too patronising, and Telling is really bad because it destroys buy-in. So I'll Coach everything.

Let's take a first look at these.

The Coaching is best myth. I love coaching – I've been a coach for 20 years. It's a major part of what I do. It's brilliant! But 'the best' approach to development?! What nonsense!

Coaching is a powerful development approach – but it's one of many. 'Coaching is best' is a myth that can lead us to try to coach everything all the time, without checking if it's the best tool for a particular job, person or context. Coaching is designed to help us think (in order to change our approach or behaviour). It's particularly designed to generate *new* thinking. Often, managers waste energy using coaching to generate new thinking about mundane fix-it task stuff (because it's supposed to be the best). Don't waste your energy – save it for those times when new thinking is needed.

The | Telling doesn't create buy-in; coaching does (which is why it's so good) | myth

What nonsense! Coaching itself doesn't create buy-in.
There's a long list of things that create buy-in when you do them well:

- Listening
- Understanding
- Creating rapport (connecting)
- Acknowledging people's personal goals
- Letting people *think things through* for themselves, or *try things out* for themselves

All of these things *are* delivered during good coaching. But they can also be delivered during other development approaches: Selling, Teaching and Telling.

When coaching's done well, it *will* create buy-in. But this isn't *because* it's coaching – it's because of the skilful behaviours of the developer. Those skilful behaviours can create buy-in whether or not we're using coaching as the development approach.

The Telling is bad myth. I don't know about you, but I get fed up when people have the answer to what I should do, but won't tell me because they believe Telling is bad. I get fed up when, rather than tell me, they start to indulge in 'crap coaching'. Crap coaching is a technical term for those interactions where the person working with you knows exactly what they want you to think, say and do, but they won't tell you. Instead, they ask an endless list of questions – trying to get you to come up with what they're thinking. Worse than this, they aren't satisfied with the answers you come up with; they keep firing in questions until you come up with the answer they already had in mind (even though they refuse to tell you this because "Telling is bad"). That's crap coaching.

Crap coaching is hugely inferior to skilful Telling. Skilful Tell and skilful Coach are equally valuable, but not for the same reasons and not always in the same situations.

Telling isn't bad. It's great when it's done well. It provides simple clarity when most needed. It can produce relief and confidence in the person being developed. It can enable people to get on with things quickly, so that they can discover the big skills they need help with. But, like coaching, its usefulness depends on the creation of productive conditions between developer and person being developed, i.e. it depends on quality listening, empathy, rapport, etc. The conditions created by the presence of these skills will affect how usefully the Tell is received.

The **Teaching is patronising** myth. This is pretty much the same as 'Coaching is best'. Teaching *can* be patronising, it's true. Teaching can be patronising when it's delivered in a patronising manner (and this, again, depends on the quality of listening, empathy and rapport used).

Skilful Teaching produces clarity, immediate skill improvement and neurological changes, which make it a powerful learning method. By the way, when I talk about Teach or Teaching, I'm not talking about lecturing. I'm not talking about someone standing at the front of a classroom communicating information – I'm not talking about the profession of teaching. I'm talking about a very particular structure and flow of communication, which is used to impart information. This is important because you might be a teacher – professionally – and never use the Teach structure that I'll describe, e.g. I notice often in the training room that I'm teaching, but I'm not using the Teach structure, and this has big implications for the effectiveness of the development I'm providing.

Autopilot often arises because of one or more of these related myths: Teaching is patronising, whereas Coaching is the best because it creates buy-in; and Telling is the worst because it doesn't create buy-in.

Often, these primary ways of thinking... *Time, Not enough skill, Lack of intention, Not even looking, Autopilot...*are bound together so tightly that it's impossible to know which one is really causing any manager to fail to develop their people.

This book will challenge you to:

1 Attack your current thinking and approach to development, and what you believe to be the 'best' approach.

2 Find a way to get on with it – actually develop people, rather than waiting 'til you've got all the task stuff sorted before you sort your people.

3 Shift out of autopilot – be more varied in your approach; be more interesting; and be more successful with your people.

4 Be more informed and thoughtful about the best approaches to take, based on the individual, the situation and the progress they've made so far – be more aware that your favourite approach isn't necessarily the best.

5 Take such little time doing it that you *will* have enough time.

My guitar teacher Paul

My guitar teacher is ace. I haven't done much of a survey here – I confess he's the only guitar teacher I've had. However, I've listened to friends describe their guitar teachers to me, and I've experienced up to a dozen music teachers over the years. My guitar teacher is ace – for me.

In truth, he's not a teacher – he is, instead, a well-rounded and skilful developer. Typically, he begins my lesson as a guitar Coach – asking me what I want now, what the direction should be for the lesson. Once we've found a direction for the lesson, he might teach me something that I want or need in order to progress in that direction. Meanwhile, he'll keep Telling me things – simple instructions about how to do something or how to improve a particular action I'm using or *the way I'm thinking* about what I'm doing.

Occasionally, he uses Coach again to help me find a way to improve a particular action I'm using ("How might you do that action differently?"). But this is rare because I don't really have enough skill or experience so far to make such a coaching approach work.

Once in a while, he'll suggest something that's not obviously relevant to the direction I've chosen. When he does this, he observes my response, notices immediately if I'm not too keen and starts to Sell it a little. He reminds me why he's suggesting it, how it works and the benefits it'll bring, and pushes me to do this thing that I'm not so keen on. He's brilliant.

A lesson with him is full-on development – it's not characterised by any one approach. It's underpinned by exceptional listening and connection with me on the basis of my own goals, interests, opinions and preferences.

I know that, as I develop, at some point he'll do more coaching of the "How might you do that action differently?" type. When he knows that I have enough experience and skill to have different options available, he'll want me to come up with these myself.

If he were to read this book, he'd probably notice that Selling is not his natural preference. He backs off quite quickly when I resist a suggestion and doesn't put too much energy into Selling it to me. If he was to develop his approach further, it might be in Selling.

But, just for the record, Paul, I don't need you to. You're brilliant!

This is what this book is about; it's about creating this dynamic, interesting and personalised development that will actually make a difference to people. It's about stopping operating in a one-dimensional, one-track manner led by nonsensical myths like those we've explored.

Chapter Three

Autopilot: its significance – why we're drawn to it and why it isn't so helpful

Let's consider in detail one of our five recurring issues that stop us developing people well.

Managers and leaders tend to install sameness; they like words such as routine, consistency, compliance, regularity. It's easy to start doing things with people the same way all the time – in the name of consistency. Even when we're not consciously trying to deliver consistency, it's easy to get one-dimensional. We get stuck – we talk to people in the same way, we try to persuade them of things in the same way, we lead them through the thinking process we always use. We settle into a kind of autopilot.

Of course, autopilot is very useful for making sure things like standards and procedures are in place. But an autopilot approach to developing people is not so good. So why do we do it? Why do some of us always choose the same manner in which to try to help people develop? Here's why:

It's easier.

We have an innate drive to preserve energy. The brain's fuel is glucose and, unconsciously, we go to great lengths to make sure we don't waste it. Once we've learned to do something, once we feel comfortable doing it and we believe it works, this innate drive to preserve our brain-fuel pushes us to stick with the approach we know.

It's easier and more fuel-efficient – even though it may not be the best way to approach the situation.

Meanwhile, on the receiving end of development, our brains and attention craves novelty to stimulate our alertness – useful states for learning and development. The brains and attention of the people you talk to will naturally go to sleep if they hear and see things presented in the same way all the time.

Consistency is always good

VS

Consistency is the enemy of attention and interest

Consistency is the enemy of learning

Always being coached isn't good. It can be boring, patronising and frustrating when you just want someone's opinion or perspective, but what you get instead is another question. You can start to wonder if they're a real person at all – whether they have their own views.

And then there's the crap coaching I've already described: when you know they have an opinion – you see it in the way they move their head and hold their mouth, you hear it in the tone of their voice – but they just keep asking crap questions, to get you to come up with the opinion they already have. In truth, it's not really coaching at all – it's just a bizarre game the developer is playing (albeit with the best of intentions).

When someone's stuck in autopilot coaching, it would be more honest, have more integrity and be a blessed relief if they would just tell us what's on their mind.

Mind you, *always* being told isn't any better. It's relentless, patronising and can be frustrating. Wouldn't it be good if someone would help you think (rather than always assuming they know what's best for you)?

Remember that idea, attributed to Einstein, which defines insanity as "doing the same thing over and over again, but expecting different results"? When we receive the same interaction over and over, it doesn't matter to us that this type of interaction (e.g. coaching) is great – a number of things begin to happen just because of the sameness.

- We groan inwardly as soon as we suspect what's coming.
- We start to go through the motions – we respond in line with what we expect is coming.
- Our brains go to sleep – we stop thinking. We hear or see the cue for the usual approach and we go into a kind of procedural state, where we're not really thinking at our best.
- Sometimes we feel an urge to resist the sameness. So, we begin to construct defences – an unconscious response to not being understood, not being treated like an individual, and being treated instead like a formula or procedure.

Any approach will get boring if it's the only one you use.

It doesn't have to be this way. If the developer is genuinely engaged and curious about what we're thinking and doing – if they listen and pay attention – if they, themselves, don't start to function procedurally in autopilot, then we will remain engaged and in a productive state.

Here's the idea:

Coach-Sell-Teach-Tell™

It's a way of thinking and acting to make sure you don't induce insanity or boredom – a way of thinking and acting to make sure you vary your approach for the benefit of the learner, and for the benefit of yourself.

Here's how it works.
1   Take only small amounts of time to develop people.
2   Don't try to sort everything in one go.
3   Don't overindulge in the amount of communication you do.
4   Get out of autopilot.
5   Pay attention to what's actually needed – thinking, skill, instruction or an irresistible push to get on with it.
6   Pick the approach that will actually work – so that the person develops.
7   Conversely, don't worry if you pick the wrong approach – keep your time investment short and it won't matter.
8   As you get more information, you can try a different approach.

The benefits?

- Your people will remain engaged.
- You can overcome their objections with your different approaches.
- You'll save yourself time.

- Your more skilled people will get better at their tasks.
- Their results, and yours, will improve.
- Interested? Then let's dive in...

Chapter Four

Coach-Sell-Teach-Tell™

Each of the four development approaches is purposeful. Each has a different objective. Each responds to a different need in the person you're developing.

I've read books before that recommend different approaches. Some of them identify a particular order to use them in, depending on the experience and skill level, attitude or performance of the person you're developing, e.g. Teach first, then when they're ready Coach, then proceed to Tell...and so on.

This isn't really the way I see it.

There isn't a cast-iron correct way of working with somebody based on set criteria, e.g. if they're wearing red socks and it's a Tuesday, then I'll coach. With development, people don't really have a predictable start and end point for the thinking and skills they have – and, therefore, your ability to predict their skill level, based on their length of time and technical knowledge in the role, can be quite low. For example, two people the same age, who seem to have identical life experience and work history, and who've attended the same workshops and read the same books about listening skills, can have remarkably different levels of listening skills. Similarly, someone who demonstrates great listening capability in one situation (with one group of people) can demonstrate a surprisingly poor level of listening capability in another, though their length of time in the role and their knowledge doesn't change.

To select a suitable place to begin developing someone, first you need that intention to change them. Then you really need to be looking...and listening – you need to observe. You need to see and hear their skill level in a particular situation and assess the best way to work with them based on your observation (rather than based on some predetermined assumption about their knowledge, experience, performance and capability). Assumptions about their knowledge, experience, etc. are useful. They're useful in preparing your thinking, but they're never as useful as what you actually see, hear and experience in the person concerned in a specific situation.

Your intention to develop someone, and then your ability to observe and scrutinise their attitude, skills, behaviours, habits and thinking in a specific situation, is vital. It's vital because it will drive your selection of the best way to work with them.

But I don't have time

Don't worry – you do – because you don't need much.

But what if I get it wrong?

Relax – it's no big deal. The only impact is wasted time and effort for you and the person you're developing. The key to this is to minimise the time and energy you put into any one interaction – this way you minimise the time and energy you waste (if it really is waste).

Right now, though, let's take a first look at distinctions between each approach – how each responds to different situations or different states in the individual you have the intention to develop.

Chapter Five

Coach

Coaching drives *thinking* – thinking designed to give the person *clarity* about something they want to do and the particular way they want to do it. This is on the basis that the person already has the know-how to get on and do it.

- Either they have this know-how naturally.
- Or they've used it in a different situation (but not here).
- Or they've used it in similar situations, but something about the current situation is causing a *block in their thinking* – and preventing them from using it here.

So, it's designed to generate *new thinking*, which will remove blocks, enabling use of existing skill.

Crucially, it's designed to make sure the person thinks things through for themselves. We're well beyond buy-in here. When we think things through for ourselves we construct the necessary hardware in our own brain to make our new approach – our new behaviour – possible. If we don't think it through for ourselves we may not actually be able to do it because our brain is just not ready.

Coaching is a two-way communication process. You're both involved.

It has a logical structure, and this guides the coach to move the coachee from one type of thinking to another. This is the fundamental role of the coach:

> I manage the thinking structure that allows the individual to use their skills better or in a different situation

There are many different coaching structures available. The one I like best for its simplicity and power moves the individual's thinking through:

1   What they want, and what this will do for them (their own goal and outcome).
2   What they've tried so far (in order to get what they want).
3   What they could try instead – generating different ideas.
4   What they're actually going to do.

Typically, it proceeds via the coach asking a question, then listening and observing while the coachee responds. Following the response, the coach either holds the silence and listens, waiting for more, or listens and asks another question – moving the individual through the thinking structure.

Many think coaching is driven by questions and that:

> I need to come up with loads of questions

> The more I ask, the more I'm coaching

> I need to come up with clever questions

> I need the magic question that will develop the person

No. This is not the case.

> Coaching is driven by quality listening

and

> Structured thinking

The coach needs to ask only enough questions to keep the thinking going. This could be none! The coach doesn't necessarily even need to understand what the individual is saying – the only person who really needs to understand is the person being developed.

As a ratio, the coach might talk for less than 5% of the time, with 95%+ talking done by the coachee.

The objectives of coaching are based on the premise that the individual already has know-how:

- To get them clear about what they want and how they want to get on with it – the clearer they get, the more likely they are to make it happen.

  Or

- To remove those internal thinking blocks they've put up, so that they can go and get on with it, using their existing know-how.

So, observe the individual. Watch, listen, talk to them and decide whether they have enough of the know-how that's needed. If you decide they do, then Coach is a good place to begin to help them get clarity about what they want (their goal). If they don't have much of the know-how required, or if you want them to get more skilful quickly, then Coach may not be the best place to begin. You may be better beginning with Sell, Teach or Tell.

If you've seen or heard a rough approximation of the necessary skills from them previously, or in a different situation, but for some reason they don't use these skills in this particular situation, coaching is a great place to begin. Coaching may be all that's needed – and not much coaching at that.

This is a first crucial reason to make sure you consciously observe the people you intend to develop – paying attention to what you're seeing and hearing in their behaviour. Ask yourself, "Do they already have enough know-how for me to begin developing them with coaching?"

Of course, you have to have that intention to develop them in the first place. This is the purpose that drives you to observe them properly.

So, in summary, Coach is about:

- Driving thinking – new thinking.
- Driving clarity – about what they want (their goal).
- Driving clarity about the way they want to do it.
- Getting them so clear that they go and get on with it.
- Noticing blocks in thinking. Working on these blocks so that they're able to use the know-how (the skills) they already have.

Helpfully, Coach doesn't require you to have the know-how yourself. It doesn't require you to have the skill to do the thing they want to do – in fact, it's irrelevant. There's every possibility that the person you're developing will go beyond your skill level anyway.

Chapter Six

Sell

This is very different from coaching. It's not about generating thinking; it's about persuasion. It uses a high level of *drive* to *push* the individual concerned to try what *you* suggest. It's about learning from experience, i.e. thinking it through for themselves happens when they try what you suggest.

Sell is a two-way communication process for developing someone.

There are many Sell structures available. So, if you've got one you like already, use it. The one I like is based on the Persuasive Selling Format made famous by Procter & Gamble, learned and used by so many of its salespeople. It proceeds via the developer making a series of statements:

1   A description of the situation the individual finds themselves in.
2   A recommendation on what to do.
3   A description of how to do it.
4   A description of the benefits of the recommended approach.
5   All this is accompanied by continuous 'closes' ("Yes?" "Yes?" "Interested?") – getting the learner nodding. And a full close at the end ("Going to give it a go?" "Yes?" "When?" "Now?").

Let's estimate that 90%+ of the active communication is by the developer, i.e. they do most of the work. It's a mistake to assume there's nothing coming from the person being developed because of that crucial element of 'closing' – getting them to say 'yes', getting them to show you verbally and non-verbally (through nods) that they're going to do what you suggest. This verbal and non-verbal agreeing should happen consistently through a good development Sell – hence the 10% from them.

It's highly structured, so that the developer doesn't go on and on – carried away by their own enthusiasm. The structure provides a beginning, middle and end; it's linear and the addition of each part is designed to make the argument more persuasive.

It's not concerned with whether the person involved has the necessary know-how; it uses a mindset of: **We'll find out later**

Key objectives for using Sell are:

- To get things moving – to get the individual moving.
- To have the individual try something – and try something right now or very soon.

As a result, it's really about:

- Pushing the individual to learn from different approaches or experiences.

With Sell the developer needs a certain proportion of the know-how. Actually, it's not know-how – it's just knowledge. You're selling a particular approach and to be persuasive, and make sense, you need to know how that approach works. You don't have to be good at it yourself – you may never have done it, or you may have done it, but you're rubbish at it. Regardless, you need enough knowledge to describe your recommendation and how it works.

Observation is vital, but not for the same reason as with Coach. You're not assessing know-how; instead, your intention is to spot the thing – the approach, the behaviour, the magic – that you believe they need to demonstrate. If you're going to be really helpful, you'll observe well enough to be able to describe exactly how this behaviour would look and sound.

So, Sell is about:

- Driving learning via experience.
- Driving new behaviour (or skill development) by pushing the person to try something different.

It's not led by thinking – it's designed to run them over with your suggestion and persuade them to have a go.

But you do need to know what you want them to try – you need to be able to describe it to them.

Chapter Seven

Teach

Teach is the approach we observe being used the least. It provides clarity about what to do and how to do it. And, significantly, it follows this clarity of information with powerful neurosurgery. It gets the brain of the learner sorted so that they have the mental hardware needed to do the new behaviour required; it makes sure they've experienced it (not just thought it through, but also *done* it – *felt* it for themselves). It finesses and refines new behaviour, beginning its transformation in the brain from something I just 'do' sometimes to something I know how to do whenever I want, i.e. a skill.

Teach is a two-way communication process for developing someone.

It proceeds via the developer:
1   Giving clarity about what's required and how to do it.
2   Giving a demonstration of how to do what's been described.
3   Getting the person involved to demonstrate it for themselves.
4   Giving feedback and further demonstrations as needed to get the person involved to finesse their ability to demonstrate it for themselves.
5   Assessing when the individual can do it well enough.
6   And at the point when they can do it well enough:
7   Getting the person involved to demonstrate it several times – cementing the '*correct*' performance and beginning to move it from the brain's conscious thinking areas to its habit centres.

It's impossible to know the participation percentage of developer and learner with Teach – it will be different every time. But our mindset (our intention) should be that it's something like a fifty/ fifty split.

Teach is highly structured. Each step has an important function for learning and transfer of learning. Each step has neurological significance – it does something different and important in the learner's brain. Whereas each step of the Sell structure is designed to make the communication more persuasive, each step of the Teach structure is designed to make it more likely that the learner *can* implement the behaviour targeted. In fact, each step makes it more difficult for them to resist doing the behaviour – because it's moved to the brain's habit centre.

Teach usually assumes the person involved does *not* have the necessary know-how, or the necessary *level* of know-how, required.

Key objectives for using Teach are:

- To make new behaviours happen immediately.
- To provide a base level of skill, upon which the developer and the individual can build.
- To make sure new behaviours can be transferred into the live situation that's relevant.
- To move the learner from a behaviour ('something I did once') to a skill ('something I know how to do') as soon as possible.
- To move the learner to a new skill level (in something where they already have some skill).

With Teach, you, the developer, need a proportion of the know-how. Similarly to Sell, it's not so much know-how as knowledge of how the approach, the behaviour and the skill you're after from the individual concerned will look, sound and feel. It can help if you have done it yourself – and therefore can pass on your own knowledge, behaviour and skill. But, if you haven't done it yourself it doesn't mean you can't use Teach; however, it's crucial that you can spot and validate the behaviour or skill you're after in the individual concerned if and when they demonstrate it.

The responsibility with Teach lies more with the developer than the learner; as a minimum, you're the judge of the behaviour the person demonstrates. It's about the level of behaviour or skill that *you're after* – which *you judge* is required from them.

Observation is doubly vital with Teach. You're assessing the level of know-how the individual already has *and* trying to spot the approach, the behaviour and the magic you believe they need to demonstrate. If you're to be helpful, you'll observe them well enough to be able to describe this behaviour in the situations in which you've observed them.

So, Teach is about:

- Helping someone to adopt new behaviours immediately.
- Turning those behaviours into repeatable know-how through practice.
- Doing so in a manner that makes small but significant changes in the brain of the learner, so they know they can use their new behaviour in the situations required.

It's not so much about thinking or persuasion; it's about clarity through seeing, hearing and then feeling for themselves the behaviour needed.

Chapter Eight

Tell

Tell is easy to do, but tricky to do well in a manner that's truly helpful. Well delivered Tell provides clarity about what to do and how to do it. Well delivered Tell gives the learner clarity of what they'll do, possibly of what they'll say and the kind of effect they're aiming to produce with these behaviours.

It's a one-way communication process for developing someone.

It proceeds via the developer:

1   Suggesting a behaviour that they want the learner to use.
2   Giving clarity about what they want to see the learner doing (how they stand, how they move).
3   Giving clarity about what they want to hear the learner saying (words and vocal qualities to use, e.g. pace, tone, volume).
4   Giving clarity about the 'feel' they want the learner to create (the kind of impact they want e.g. confidence, warmth, impact, inclusiveness, etc).

That's it – now they stand back and let the learner get on with it.

Of course, we can expect the learner to nod and give small vocal signals of agreement or disagreement. But, if we ignore these tiny contributions, Tell is unapologetically 100% the developer.

If you look back at the way Tell proceeds, you can see it operates on a continuum from very little structure (if you stop at the end of number one) to a solid basic structure (if you complete steps one to four). Each of the four steps adds clarity. There's nothing in the Teller's behaviour to make their instructions more persuasive (that's Sell). There's nothing promoting thinking (that would be Coach), there's nothing promoting the practise of the behaviours (that would be Teach). So, this structure makes for a very clean, direct and straightforward communication – and this is its power.

When using Tell, there's no assumption about whether or not the learner has the know-how required; it's not really relevant. Like Sell, it's designed to make something happen now. When done well, Tell provides such straightforward information and clarity about what to do and how to do it that the assumption is it *will work*. Whether or not the learner has the necessary know-how at the moment, they'll have it (they'll find it) once they implement the developer's instructions.

Key objectives for using Tell are:

- To make new behaviours happen immediately.
- To provide such simple instruction about such small chunks of behaviour that the individual will be able to do them immediately.
- To help the learner learn via experience.

As a developer using Tell, you have to know what you're after and have an idea how to do it. You don't need to be able to do it yourself, but you have to be able to describe it specifically enough that the learner can follow your instruction. If you have done it yourself, you can pass on your own knowledge, behaviour and skill. If you haven't done it yourself, you have to be able to state what it is you want regardless (so it's still possible – you might have seen exactly how someone else does it).

A large proportion of responsibility for the approach – whether it will work, and whether it's even appropriate – stays with the developer, since the learner is following the developer's instructions. If for any reason what they do fails or causes problems for them, the developer needs to be there to support them – ultimately, the developer needs to share the responsibility for the outcome. And for this reason, Tell has an element of danger attached.

Observation is vital before Tell. You're assessing the level of know-how the individual already has *and* trying to spot the approach, the behaviour and the magic you believe they need to demonstrate. You need to base your instructions on a sound understanding of the situation and how the suggested behaviour will fit into it. Again, this is only responsible if you're going to be so direct as to Tell.

So, Tell is about:

- Creating an immediate change in behaviour.
- Simplicity and clarity of what to do and how to do it.
- Sensory clarity – what the developer wants to see, hear and feel from the learner.
- Lack of discussion – an assumption the learner will implement the instruction and learn from it.
- Brevity – it's short, and it's clean and simple.

Chapter Nine

Your intention to develop

I listed a lack of intention to develop as one of the primary barriers that mean managers accidentally keep a lid on the capability level of their workforce. Let's consider this issue for a moment.

Intention can take you a long way in people development. So many managers, leaders, trainers and coaches we work with don't have this intention to work *on* the person. They have an intention to get tasks done, or make others get tasks done, but they don't have an intention to *change* the person delivering those tasks – to *move* their thinking or behaviour from one place to another.

You may not like this idea of changing the person who's delivering those tasks. You may think I shouldn't change people but that's what development is.

Development is about change

Even if you insist on some linguistic mindset trick like I'm here to make more of people's strengths don't kid yourself – it's still about change, trying to get something different to happen via a different behaviour, different use of the same behaviour or an increase in skill. These changes don't happen in isolation – they change the person. Check yourself now – are you happy to change people? If you're not, then you may not be a developer. And if you're a manager, a trainer, a coach or a teacher, it may be that you're not going to be a very good one if you're not happy to change people.

This mindset regarding changing people is one to get past quickly – it's not as extreme as it sounds. If you're to help people change successfully, then it won't really be you who changes them; they'll choose to change themselves. You'll work in a way where you'll get their permission to help them change, and they'll choose to change because of your intention and the work you do with them.

My guitar teacher has the intention to change me – with my permission. Let's be clear: he doesn't turn up every week to check whether I've practised my scales and arpeggios, but every lesson he arrives with the intention to change me from non-guitarist, into rubbish guitarist, into mediocre guitarist, into average guitarist, into good guitarist. And, whatever that means in terms of the way he needs to help me rearrange my thinking, my behaviours, my skills and my approach, he'll do it. Can you imagine how useless a guitar teacher would be without this intention?

Now imagine how useless a manager is without this intention. Imagine how useless a trainer is without this intention. Imagine how useless an HR partner is without this intention. Imagine how useless a teacher is without this intention.

Just check whether you have enough intention to change the people who work for you, the people who work with you and the people who want development from you. This is important because it's only the presence of this intention that will mean you're actually observing the person involved – observing them as a person – and seeing the skill or behaviour they need your help to affect. Without this intention, you may only observe whether the **task** gets done sufficiently well.

Once you've got the intention, ask yourself whether you know how you want the person you're working with to think or behave. Often we find managers know they want people to be different, but they haven't worked out how. This is the significance of observing. But, even when observing, you'll have to remind yourself regularly that your intention is to develop the **individual** and that you need to pay attention to them – to their behaviours and their thinking – otherwise you may find you drift straight back into observation and opinions about the task only.

Chapter Ten

Time

Coach

Once I asked a group of thirty customer services managers how long coaching takes. To a person, they agreed twenty minutes. Twenty minutes!?! Each of them had between five and twenty-five people on their team whom they needed to develop. With a mindset like this, they were *unlikely* to do much coaching in a week – certainly less than one session a day. If you think it takes twenty minutes to coach someone, you won't find the time to coach many people.

Coaching requires twenty minutes

I don't have twenty minutes

I can't coach

I need to tell

It doesn't have to be this way. In terms of investment of energy and time for you both, coaching can be quick – if you stay disciplined, a good coaching session can be delivered at the coffee machine in as little as one to five minutes. But because it drives thinking – encourages thinking by providing a little space – it's tempting to allow coaching to take longer. Much longer. So, you may find it tricky to keep it to five minutes. Keep this in mind. This is *your* limitation – not the limitation of coaching as an approach.

Sell ▶

The point of Selling is to be quick. Your Sell should communicate energy and speed – the point is to run over the learner with the *push* to try something. With Sell you're not promoting discussion or debate – you're pushing for "yes", "of course" and "let me at it" from the learner. Since there's a risk of the approach or idea you sell not working, it's really not worth investing much time. Run them over, get them to try your recommendation, then pick up again with some reflection time afterwards.

If Coach can be delivered in as little as five minutes, Sell can be as short as three. The trick is to identify a small enough chunk of information or behaviour that you're looking to "sell". If you take longer, it's possible you've picked a chunk of information that is too big or your discipline is at fault again.

Over-selling is an example of a lack of discipline. If you don't get a "yes" – nods and affirmations that the learner is with you and wants to try your suggestion – the temptation is to keep going. You add in more detail, indulge in debate and explore barriers and obstacles stopping the individual (these last ones are a switch into Coach). Don't do this. Stop, back off and leave it for another time.

This is the most difficult thing to do! This is the thing that requires discipline from the developer. It's vital, because engaging in discussion and further reasoning – trying to come up with more persuasive arguments – is where your time will go. And when you invest this further time and it still doesn't work – the learner still doesn't adopt the new behaviours you're suggesting – then you'll feel like you've wasted your time. This feedback loop won't motivate you to provide more development.

This doesn't only apply to Sell; when you perceive the learner isn't responding in the way you want, it's easy to lose discipline whichever method you use. Look out for common mindsets like:

I can fix this person   I need to fix this person

and   I need to fix them now

I must sort out everything at once

I must complete their development right now

Let's be clear about the time trap here: it's a circular thought pattern that kills your ability to provide enough development. This is how it works:

1   You start by believing that developing people takes lots of time – too much – time you don't have.

2   Next, you try some development, but you're not disciplined:

   a) You like the sound of your own voice too much.

   b) You try to "fix" everything at once.

   c) You're desperate to make a difference – so you're complete about what needs to be covered.

   d) When the learner resists, you try to overcome their objections. When they continue to resist, you keep going – you get into a discussion, a debate even.

   e) When they continue to resist, you switch from one method to another without considering whether you should, e.g. you switch from Sell (three minutes) into Coach (five minutes), then back into Sell (another three minutes), then back into Coach again (another five minutes), and then, finally, in frustration, you switch into an ineffective Tell (one minute).

3   The whole thing takes too long – it stops you completing other urgent work you have to do.

4   You remind yourself that development takes too long (you knew it was true!).

5   You avoid development conversations – you know they will take more time than you have.

6   You don't do any development because it takes too much time.

Do yourself a favour – move your mindset:

From: To:

| I must fix this person |

| Make small improvements |

| Just get them moving |

| I must cover everything now |

| Just get them moving |

| Create many small changes over time |

| I must get it right |

| Fast not perfect |

| More time spent = more learning |

| Quality interventions = more learning |

| Amount of time is irrelevant |

This is the secret of success. Crucially, if *you* allow *yourself* to take too much time, you'll never want to provide development.

Teach

There's more involved with Teach. It's perfectly reasonable to expect it to take longer. As with Sell, identify small enough chunks of behaviour to Teach – this will help – along with the personal discipline that we've touched on above. Think five to ten minutes for Teach, depending on the size of the chunk you work on.

Tell

Clearly, this is the shortest – it's designed to be brief and direct, and bypass discussion. Again, your personal discipline is what enables this. Even if you deliver all four stages, covering what you want to see, hear and feel, you should be aiming at only one or two minutes. More than this and you're certainly attempting too much at once.

In summary, your intention with each could be:
Coach – five minutes
Sell – three minutes
Teach – ten minutes
Tell – one minute

It's only a mindset or an intention – it's not anything like as precise a science as this implies. The significant thing is to *be able* to achieve this short development – this will enable your intention to develop. If you know *you can* keep your development sessions short, you'll know you can afford time. Studies demonstrate that, for all kinds of reasons, multiple short hits over a long period of time are much more likely to produce change than a massive indulgence once every few months.

Chapter Eleven

How it works

Here's the broad idea we'll cover through the rest of the book:

1   Get your connection first – so that the individual you want to develop buys in to your help.

2   Good listening drives a large part of your ability to get this connection. Good listening requires you to inhibit or "stop" your impulse to jump in too early, to offer empathy, sympathy, opinions and insight.

3   Observe – take small amounts of time to watch and listen to what the learner does, in order to assess the development you believe they need. By small, I mean a number of two-minute observations.

4   Observe – once you know what they need, you can continue to observe to decide whether they already know enough, whether they already have some skill that will help them to achieve the development they need. You'll use this to decide on the approach to take first. If they already have some appropriate skill, then Coach suggests itself as your approach immediately; if they don't, then Sell-Teach-Tell suggest themselves. Now you can consider how important it is that they get it right first time (Teach), how little time you have yourself (Sell-Tell), how important it is to just get them moving (Sell), or how simple and clear you can be (Tell).

5   Get started – Coach-Sell-Teach or Tell. But keep it short – know that, whatever you do, there's a chance it won't work on this first and subsequent occasions. It's a journey, so it's more

important to get started than it is to try to complete it. Be clear with yourself that the development you provide is *unlikely* to work first time; stick with your time disciplines – one minute, three minutes or ten minutes. Don't go beyond this – development and learning aren't increased by the amount of time you spend on them in one go; they are increased by the quality of the interaction, the quality of the method used. The 10,000 hours that's currently emphasised as important doesn't take people to mastery because of the number of hours; instead, this amount of time allows individuals to learn in multiple ways and in different contexts. It's not the 10,000 itself – it's the quality of learning experience that 10,000 hours brings. As a developer, *you're* not expected to provide the 10,000 hours – that's for the learner to do. Your job is to put quality interventions into their 10,000 hours of practice – and, once again, the length of time of your intervention doesn't imply quality.

6   Observe – take further short amounts of time to watch and listen to what they do now, as a result of your first intervention. Are they doing things any differently?

7   Keep going – Coach-Sell-Teach-Tell™ in response to what you see now. Switch techniques if their progress implies this might help. If, for example, you've taught them something and you can see now they have a different level of skill, but they're struggling to use it, it will make sense to switch from Teach to Coach.

8   Observe some more – further short amounts of time.

9   Keep going – decide when they can cope with you building the next level of skill or behaviour on top of what they're now demonstrating, *and* when you can move on from the skill you began with to something completely different.

Chapter Twelve

Connection

If you want the development you provide to create change in the individual you're working with, building rapport between you first is key. "Rapport" is from the French *"en rapport"*, which means "in connection".

You need this connection so that the person you're developing has an implicit trust in you, listens to you and will follow the direction your development suggests. It doesn't mean they'll do whatever your development requires, but it means they commit to the relationship enough to consider what's required (it means they won't just reject what you do with them). They'll stay committed to the development even if they decide not to do all the things you work on together.

Connection is the basis of a good relationship. It's about doing things – speaking, moving, thinking – in ways that give the person you're developing a sense that "you're my kind of person". Or, at the very least, the sense that "you know where I'm coming from". It doesn't arise because you agree with what they say or what they do (although this is certainly a route to connection); instead, it arises because the way you're saying things and the way you're doing things is in some ways similar to the way they speak and the way they behave – and therefore it appeals to them.

Building a good connection with some people may take you quite a lot of work because they're so unlike you, or because you just don't like the way they speak and behave. But, as a general rule, it takes a lot less work than we often believe. So many managers and developers tell me it'll take weeks and months of working together for them to have a good enough relationship to really challenge the person they're developing. This isn't correct. Sometimes it can take no more than a few minutes.

Sometimes it's as simple as spending a little time:

- Smiling when they smile.
- Stopping smiling when they're not smiling (i.e. not pushing your happiness upon them).
- Listening well to them, so that they know you're listening.
- Agreeing with something they're saying (even something small).
- Acknowledging what they're saying, even if you disagree with it. Then resisting the temptation to comment on it or disagree with it (i.e. let them see you've heard, you've understood and you're still thinking about what they've said).

Once you have a good connection, you'll be able to be more challenging. You'll be able to disagree, you'll be able to push them more – even criticise what they're saying – and they'll stay with you (they won't reject the development you're providing, even if they're less comfortable with what you're saying or doing).

So, don't rush into development. Whether you Coach-Sell-Teach or Tell, make sure you spend some time properly listening to the individual, their perceptions, their priorities and wants, concentrating on building this connection a little before moving into development (which will test the level of connection you have). But don't take weeks and months either.

Rapport is *the* key element that creates buy-in; it creates it regardless of whether you're Coaching, Selling, Teaching or Telling. Ironically, crap coaching risks breaking your connection with someone, destroying their buy-in. Deciding you already know what you want the person to say, then asking questions to get them to say it – until they give you "the right answers" – destroys buy-in.

Once you've got connection, you need to maintain it. Keep assessing it throughout your interactions, noticing when you may have pushed things too far with your level of challenge, the force of your suggestions and the way you're putting pressure on them to have a go at what they've decided to do.

When you notice that you've pushed them too far, back off and turn down your level of challenge. Rebuild the connection.

Chapter Thirteen

Listening

Listening is the most significant skill in establishing a connection, and possibly the most significant in creating buy-in. Good listening is important regardless of the approach you take – Coach, Sell, Teach or Tell. It demonstrates that "I understand you – I get you" and this builds connection.

If I'm going to Coach you, it just won't work if I don't listen to you well. Someone listening to me is the key stimulus for me to think things through for myself. Coaching needs strong listening.

If I'm going to Sell-Teach-Tell, it's vital you know I've listened. You're less likely to try what I suggest if you don't know that I'm listening to you – without this crucial element demonstrating that I understand enough what's going on for you, and the context for what you're trying to do, then it wouldn't make sense for you to start doing things I suggest.

My two favourite methods for listening are simple – outrageously simple:

1   100% listen. This one is just an instruction to yourself to shut up
    – shut up and let the person speak, and resist your temptation to
    join the conversation for a while. It's straightforward, but that
    doesn't make it easy to do. Just yesterday, in a coaching session,
    I was overwhelmed by the amount and breadth of information
    that the person I was working with wanted to talk through.

2   Repeating back. This one takes practice. It takes time for your brain to adjust to listening with the kind of precision that it generates. But it is simple. The idea is that you don't paraphrase what you hear; instead, you literally restate the exact words that the person concerned has just said. You can do this in a number of different ways:
    - Repeat back single words.
    - Repeat back a particular phrase they've used.
    - Repeat back just two or three words of a topic or idea they're talking through (this is like summarising, but once again, the significance is that it's their words you're using).

Each time you do this, you can pause and wait to find out what they're going to do with the word or phrase that you've repeated back, e.g. they might confirm that "yes, that is what I said – that is what I meant". Or they might disagree that this is what they meant to say and find a different way to say what's on their mind. They might simply give you more thoughts – expanding on things.

Whatever they do with the words you're repeating back to them, the fact that you're using their own words should help to build the connection between you. I say "should" only because if you repeat them like a cold-hearted and mechanical robot (and they themselves are not a cold-hearted and mechanical robot), then this may not endear you to them so much.

Chapter Fourteen

Inhibiting

The big enabler in listening is something called inhibiting. It's defined as "to hinder, restrain or prevent (an action or process)". Inhibiting is one of the five executive functions of your mind – your thinking brain or prefrontal cortex. At different times and in different situations – depending on what we can see and hear around us – our ability to inhibit our impulses decreases. We need to develop it as a conscious instruction to ourselves.

There are many things you'll need to "inhibit" if you're to be successful with Coach–Sell–Teach–Tell™. Some of them we've already begun to explore, e.g. the need to inhibit my impulse "to fix" the individual, the need to get everything right first time and the need to cover everything.

In listening, there are a number of things that are crucial for you to inhibit.

The big one is your impulse to "jump in" – to start speaking yourself (rather than listen). There are lots of ways this impulse manifests itself:

- You want to empathise – finding ways to say that you understand what they're saying.
- You want to tell them that you too have experienced the thing they're describing.

- You have an opinion about what they're saying, and you want to tell them.
- You have an insight about what they're saying – it's reminded you of some key rule or principle, which has been of great benefit to you, and you want to share this with them.

And so on…

There's no hard and fast rule to help us here. Empathy, sympathy, opinion and insight are all great tools in development – they're right at the heart of Sell-Teach-Tell, and people will find them very useful. But timing is key; to do some quality listening, so that you genuinely understand and connect with the individual, you need to listen well enough first. Nobody knows how much listening will be required – it could be seconds; it could be minutes. You'll need to judge how quickly the connection is happening and how quickly you've managed to communicate that you understand what's happening for them (even if you don't). And, of course, you'll need to judge *you have actually understood* before you steam in with your empathy, sympathy, opinion and insight.

There are less positive versions of these impulses to jump in:

- Instead of empathy, it's possible you're just more interested in your own experience – it's possible you just want to get stuff off your chest.
- Instead of sympathy, it's possible that you're too interested in what they're telling you; you're getting too interested in the story – like you'd get interested in a soap opera, a novel or a movie – and you're getting involved.
- Instead of opinion, it's possible that you just love the sound of your own voice, and you love the ego trip of having a captive audience – one which has to listen to you for a few moments.
- Instead of insight, it's possible you have the impulse to show off – a different kind of ego trip – and you're just feeling

the impulse to demonstrate how much you know, or how experienced or knowledgeable you are.

Whatever your impulse, it will help if you become more skilled at inhibiting, so that you can listen better. Pay attention to yourself while you're paying attention to the person you're developing – and give yourself regular instructions:

"Shut up"   "Listen"   "Wait"

I personally use this last one a lot. I have a wonderful dog, called Rufus, and I have totally failed to teach him that roads and cars are dangerous and can harm him. Whenever we get to a kerb, I look down at him at my heel and I say to him, "WAIT." But his powers of inhibiting are particularly poor – the sight of something interesting on the other side of the road pulls at him, and the smell of something – anything – overpowers his brain and tries to pull him into the road. So one "WAIT" is never enough. I usually end up standing at the kerb looking down at him, saying "Wait… Wait… WAIT!"

Pathetically, I'm very similar to Rufus – not with the road, but with my listening. As soon as I start to get a whiff of understanding of someone's development need, I'm in danger of running straight into the road with my need to hear the sound of my own voice, and my need to "show off" my knowledge, insight and expertise. I regularly have to talk to myself while I'm listening to the person I'm developing – telling myself to "Wait… Wait… WAIT!"

Chapter Fifteen

Observation one – spotting the need

Most of the time, you'll be able to observe the learner you're working with during meetings, presentations and negotiations you're attending. But sometimes you may need to deliberately do it when there's no particular context, e.g. when they're sitting at their desk apparently working on something (whatever's happening – or not happening – will demonstrate to you something about their personal organisation).

I don't have time for this

This is a reasonable objection. You certainly don't have *much* time for this. Most people we've worked with over the last twenty years either do no observation or far too much – it's the same issue as the amount of time people spend on development.

I only need two minutes – but I need to focus

If you really have an intention to observe – to see and hear clearly what the *learner* is doing, to decide what skills you're seeing and to notice what's missing – you don't need much time at all. You'll probably spot within the first two minutes of a focused observation the behaviours or skills you want to address. You can invest a further twenty-eight minutes if you like, but it's often the case that your conclusion about what to work on will be the same as your conclusion was in the first two minutes.

In reality, then, what you really need is a number of two-minute observations, which you can spread out over a thirty-minute meeting/presentation, etc. or over a longer period of time.

By observation, I mean actually watching and listening to the person do their thing – not always jumping in yourself to make sure the outcome is achieved (saving them from their own lack of capability) and interfering in what they're attempting to do. It's difficult, but you can do it if you keep reminding yourself that you need to see how *they* do things.

Your reason for observation is to identify clearly enough what it is you intend to develop the individual in. Certainly Sell-Teach-Tell will fail without this. Strictly speaking, Coach doesn't require this same kind of observation, because with Coach you don't need to know what the skill is you're going to attempt to develop in the individual concerned. With Coach, the individual chooses the direction, the topic, and develops the how-tos from their existing experience and thinking.

Now, I can hear you thinking:

> Great – I like Coach best – I don't have to invest time in observation and I don't need to have an opinion about how this person should develop

But without observation it's difficult to know that you should choose Coach at all. You need to observe to see and hear that they've already got sufficient know-how to make Coach work well. Also, sometimes it may help to understand the context for yourself – you may be able to challenge the learner's thinking with what you understand.

There's more to consider about observation – quite a bit more – but, before that, let's take a detailed look at the first of the four approaches: Coach.

Chapter Sixteen

How to Coach

Just a brief recap first.

Coaching is designed to unlock a person's existing skills, which for some reason they're not making use of in the particular situation or context. To do this, it:

- Drives thinking – new thinking, the coachee's own thinking (to get the coachee's own brain ready for change and capable of change, getting them to think it through for themselves).
- Drives clarity – about their goal.
- Drives clarity about the way they want to do it.
- Gets them so clear that they go and get on with it.
- Gets them to notice blocks in thinking and remove or change these somehow.
- Focuses on the future – the way forward, the solution, rather than the problem, the detailed history of the problem and the causes of the problem. This is crucial in terms of how it helps people, but also in terms of how little time it can take you to help people to develop themselves.

The GROW cycle still seems to me a powerful thinking structure for managers and developers using coaching in the workplace:

Goal
Reality
Options
Will or Wrap Up

Comprehensive guides on how to use it are plentiful, so please check the references I've listed[6].

There are thousands of questions you could ask when following the GROW cycle. Often, I find that people who've received training in how to coach have been taught hundreds of these questions. They've been issued with a page of questions for each stage of the cycle. You know the kind of thing – thirty questions per page. That's easily 120 available questions as a starter.

I don't like this – it betrays a few mindsets I've mentioned before, which lead people astray with their coaching and the development they provide, for example:

Coaching is a questioning process

and

I must find the best question to unlock their thinking

These mindsets encourage the developer to keep firing in questions. They lead the developer to try to become a judo master in questioning, searching for the cleverest question that will do the job. They encourage the developer to become far too interested in the content of the coaching session – and, once they're interested, they become opinionated about how to fix the problem (they start to lead the witness). Not only does all this make Coaching in less than five minutes very challenging, it puts the developer in danger of behaving in a "smug", "know-it-all" kind of manner, which isn't at all helpful for their connection with the learner, and therefore the development of the learner.

6 John Whitmore, *Coaching for Performance*, Nicholas Brealey Publishing, 1992. Max Landsberg, *The Tao of Coaching*, Harper Collins, 1996. David Rock, *Quiet Leadership*, Harper Collins, 2006

As the developer, when Coaching, it's useful to remind yourself from time to time:

It's not about me – it's about the learner   so

Get over yourself   and   Get out of the way

It's helpful to have mindsets like:

Coaching is a listening process   and

The quality of my attention is what unlocks their thinking   and

A dozen simple questions are more than enough. After that, I must keep out of their way – let them think clearly   and

If I stick to a small number of questions, I'll remember them so easily I can just focus on listening well

And what are the dozen questions? Well, you can pick them yourself from the page-long lists of questions you received on your training course. But, if you haven't been on one, then I have ten favourites, which do the job:

Goal:	What do you want?
Reality:	Where are you up to so far?
	What have you tried so far (to get you what you want)?
	Is it working?
	So do you want to carry on with this approach, or try something different?
Options:	What could you do?
	And what else?
Will or Wrap Up:	What will you do?
	By when?
	When will you begin?

Sometimes this is all it will take. Sometimes not as much as this – sometimes just stick with these four:

- What do you want?
- What have you tried so far?
- What could you do?
- What will you do?

But, whatever the questions, they have to be accompanied by your best listening and a bit of summarising back to the learner what you've heard them say.

This is perfectly achievable in five minutes (as long as you shut up and don't build the conversation into something much bigger with your own unnecessary contributions).

I'm saying this here because, in managers we've observed over the last twenty years, their own need to make contributions has been a regular cause of coaching taking too long: *The developer gets too interested in what's being said and starts asking deeper and more insightful questions (which follow their own interest rather than the coachee's). Then they make unnecessary contributions, which increase the length of the conversation.*

I observe many developers asking just three questions:

Reality: Why's this happening?
Options: What needs to be done?
Will or Wrap Up: How will you do that?

This is ROW coaching – coaching without development of the coachee's goal. While this can be useful, it's really not coaching. The questions may be delivered in a nice respectful coaching style, but, structurally, the thought process driven by these questions is different from coaching. It's a thought process missing all kinds of essential things like *motivation, identification of the right target to shoot at, buy-in, new thinking, specifics, the possibility of step-change, action orientation and harnessing the workings of the learner's brain,* to list just a few.

Another approach that crops up frequently when managers believe they're coaching is:

Reality: What's the problem?
Will or Wrap Up: How will you fix that?

This might be useful management, but it's not coaching in two crucial ways:

1   It's not really driving thinking – new thinking, or even any thinking. It's driving action orientation, which is powerful, but not thinking. It's a different tool and it doesn't really provide any development.

2   Again, it's missing a goal – and new thinking, with all the kinds of killer implications already listed above.

Let's take a look at my ten favourite questions to make sure the significance of each one is clear.

Goal: What do you want?

"Want" is the language of goals – what the individual "wants" is owned by the individual concerned, e.g. by comparison, "need" is the language of a target; it's not always owned by the individual concerned – they *need* it in order to satisfy someone else. Getting the language of this first question correct is instrumental. Many managers are obsessed with the importance of creating buy-in, but then they miss this question. If you want to create buy-in, ask the individual you're coaching, "What do you want?" Don't fudge your language.

Reality: Where are you up to?

This question is designed to drive a quick gap analysis – getting the individual concerned to see, hear and feel that *there is* a gap and that, therefore, something needs to be done to close that gap.

Reality: What have you tried so far?

This is an unblocker and powers *new* thinking. When you get to options, it'll be useful for you both to have heard what the individual has tried already in order to get what they want. For very good reasons of energy preservation, the thinking brain can be a bit lazy; when you challenge people to come up with new approaches to situations, it's entirely normal for them to identify actions that they've already taken. So, this reality question allows you (and them) to spot this trap and avoid it. But this means you must pay attention for them – make sure you're clear on what they've tried already, so that you can point it out when they propose to try all the same stuff again.

Reality: Is it working?

This one's an unblocker as well. It's designed to get the individual clear that what they've tried so far hasn't got them what they want, and therefore something different is required. As with all answers, you'll need to listen closely to the answer they give to this one – they'll sometimes answer with things like "Sort of" and "Some of the time". Once you've acknowledged such answers (by repeating them back), you might just ask the question again, so that the individual can hear themselves say, "No – it's not working" – providing the clarity that something new is needed.

Reality: So, do you want to carry on with this approach, or try something different?

Another unblocker. It may seem a bit of an odd one, but you'll be surprised how often, despite the fact that their current approach isn't getting them what they want, an individual will still feel they should keep going with it. This isn't as weird as it appears; often, people think "Doing something is better than doing nothing". So, if they don't believe there are other approaches available, they'd rather just keep going, hoping that, for some reason, the thing they've been doing will suddenly start working.

This question gets the individual clear on the madness of carrying on doing the things they've tried before – the things that haven't worked so far. It allows them to hear themselves saying, "I want to try something different." Or, "Well, I don't know what I could do that would be different." It's *a lead into the next bit of thinking. You can reassure them, "It's OK – let's do a little bit of thinking about this now" and move into options.*

Options: What could you do?

The word "could" is vital here – you're not asking for a commitment to action yet. Answers to this question are only possibilities – at this stage, you're getting the individual to think *new thoughts*. And you're getting them to think it through for themselves – their brain is reconfiguring in front of you as they consider different approaches. You can and should repeat this question a few times, stretching their thinking to come up with several ideas; it's the availability of these different options that means they've properly thought through things for themselves.

Wrap up/Will: What will you do?

Simple, this one – just change the tense of the last question. The move from "could" to "will" generates the individual's decision – which of the possibilities they've come up with so far is the one? – and moves them from thinking into action.

Wrap up/Will: By when?/When will you begin?

Often, by this point, our brains are tired and we fudge this bit – we think everything's done, but it's not. These questions are as significant as what's come before. Make sure you keep listening. This timescale-type thinking is reconfiguring the brain around issues like urgency, possibility, whether they're really clear enough and whether they're convinced about the option they've chosen. The whole piece can still fall apart at this stage (and better that it does if the individual isn't convinced – the only real problem with this is if you've taken too much time).

It's so simple! (You may not think so after all this). Actually – it really is. If, that is, you can get out of your own way and just allow yourself to stick with these questions, listen and repeat back to help the individual keep up with what they're thinking, and maintain your connection.

Once, Doug, my business partner and sometime co-author, was talking to a client of his on the phone. As far as she was concerned, he was coaching her, except that the phone signal was coming and going, and hearing what she was saying was intermittent. Rather than interrupting her train of thought to tell her this, Doug stuck with his disciplines – repeated back those phrases, words and sentences he *could* hear, and held his silence. When he could hear that she was getting to the end of the particular part of her thinking, he'd ask the next question from the very simple structure above.

You may have guessed the punchline to this one already. At the end of the coaching session, Doug's client was very excited and enthusiastic. As they finished, she thanked him profusely and exclaimed that she thought this had probably been the best coaching session she'd ever had – this coaching session in which Doug may have heard as much as 50% of what she'd said. This is possible because Doug provided great attention and structured thinking, even though he couldn't hear the content.

Of course, this is entirely the point with Coach – get out of the way of the person you're coaching *and* get out of the way of yourself – let the combination of the structure, your quality listening and your repetition of what the individual is saying work its magic. You don't always have to understand (or even hear) what they're saying, or how they're thinking – it's their thinking after all.

Chapter Seventeen

Mindset traps in Coach

Mindset traps at Goal stage:

I don't like the answer they give me to the **Goal** question

It's not the right goal

I want to change their goal

It's tempting to challenge what the individual wants, suggest alternatives, change the words they use or just tell them they've got it wrong. As a manager, this might be a valid way of working, but if you do it often, don't kid yourself you're coaching.

When Coaching, don't do it. Stick with what the individual wants, even if it sounds really wrong. Changing what they want just means you risk nothing happening (because what needs to happen is no longer tied to what *they* want).

Stick with what they want – it will actually drive them to get on with what's needed

So much of this is about time. If I only take five minutes to Coach someone, then it's no big deal if they've got "the wrong goal'" for me.

I've wasted very little time

> Getting them thinking isn't a waste of time anyway (unless I take too long)

> I can come back to them on another day (take a different approach) once I see nothing's changing

Traps at the Reality stage revolve around *time* and *fascination*:

> I'm fascinated by what they've done

> I'm wanting to know more about their approach

> I think I understand what's wrong with the approach they've taken

If I spend too much time on Reality questions – if I get too interested in what's wrong – then I may accidentally drive them to focus on the problems, rather than drive forwards to solutions and action.

This is a valid management focus (particularly if I'm moving into performance management activity with the person concerned). But in Coaching – in development – it's surprisingly counterproductive.

The brain processes incoming information into a network of brain cells – a network of linked ideas located throughout the brain. It does this by making new neural connections between the incoming information and existing neural networks. When we talk and think through the cause of problematic behaviour, the brain makes more and more connections between the problem and different parts of the network – we actually strengthen the connections that make up the problematic behaviour. As a result, getting individuals to spend a lot of energy and time going deep into the current situation – analysing the whys and wherefores – can actually reinforce the unproductive thinking that is keeping them from getting what they want. Deep analysis of people's motivations, behaviours and responses is not the same as deep analysis of numbers or scientific data – there's rarely a black-and-white answer. And while you're exploring the problematic behaviours, attitudes and thinking they're using, you're accidentally making it more difficult for them to stop.

This is particularly tricky if it involves habitual behaviours, i.e. if people are stuck with a habit, then analytical thinking about this habit – deep thinking about why it's happening – may strengthen the habit in the brain and harden its wiring.

As a manager, and developer, you're better off leaving this kind of work to a trained therapist – stay disciplined, and don't get yourself or the individual too analytical about the problems.

Because of this, "why" questions about the cause of a situation can be particularly dangerous in development. Some coaching approaches suggest techniques like "Five Whys", i.e. ask "Why?" five times in order to get to the bottom of the problem. This may be brilliant for data-driven, or scientific, scenarios, but for problematic thinking and behaviours it can be counterproductive (though we might enjoy the pseudo-psychological insights we think we're producing).

The "why" question is a great management approach if you're simply trying to wake somebody up to their responsibility for a situation. But it may be a very bad question if you're coaching them to get their brain ready for new approaches to situations.

Remember, the Reality stage is about:

1   Getting clear that I'm not yet getting what I want.
2   Recognising what I've tried already (so I don't keep doing the same things, hoping for a different result).
3   Recognising that I may not have tried very much (so there's plenty of scope for new options).
4   Realising that my current approach hasn't been working – so new thinking is needed.

Beyond fulfilling these relatively simple functions, we may not need a Reality step at all, so be careful – don't get too interested and overdo it.

Mindset traps at Options stage:

Now I know what you want and what you've tried, I think you're barking up the wrong tree

Remember to let them think it through for themselves; don't rush into telling them their options are "wrong" or "won't work". If you're Coaching, then you've already decided that new thinking would be useful. So disagreeing with their new thinking immediately can be confusing and not so helpful! You also risk drifting out of Coaching and into debate and discussion again, which will quickly consume your time – and we know that this is counterproductive in all kinds of ways.

Have faith they'll figure it out

Repeat back each option – let them hear for themselves whether it makes sense or not.

Or   Keep their focus on their goal

Refer them back to it again and again – "Remember, this is what you want – will this get you that?" "OK, so what else could you do?"

And   Make sense of what they've already done

Keep referring them back to Reality – "You said you've tried that approach already" "So what else could you do to get a different outcome this time?"

Mindset traps at Will/Wrap Up:

> The coaching's finished – this bit's easy

> The thinking is over; this is about action

These mindsets can lead you to fudge the specifics of actions and timescales for those actions.

> Turning could-dos into will-dos is essential thinking

When considering timescales, the learner is still thinking it all through for themselves in a significant manner. So be picky about the "what" and the "when". Don't accept lazy thinking, e.g. in answer to "When will you begin?" learners can say lazy things like "Immediately." Since they've done quite a bit of thinking already (even in five minutes), their thinking brains are tired.

> Keep them on it now – be annoying if necessary

You need to use the rapport you've built so far to keep them thinking clearly at this crucial moment.

If they say something like "Immediately" or "Today," you need to repeat back again and check it's true, e.g. "Really? Tomorrow? Are you in tomorrow?" This continuation of thinking is getting their brain really clear about what and when – making it real – and wiring it into the neural network they'll use, so stay on it.

None of this needs to take more than five minutes. If you don't get too interested, if you don't start adding in your own thoughts, if you stop yourself asking more and more questions, you'll find that five minutes is often a huge amount of time for this productive, disciplined Coaching.

Chapter Eighteen

Observation two – managing your own attention

Since most of your observation of the person you're developing will be in a meeting, a presentation or an interaction you're taking part in yourself, you'll need to manage where you point your eyes and ears.

Remember, your conscious brain finds it difficult to focus on too many things at once. One person talking takes up at least half of your brain's attention capacity – trying to focus on two different conversations at one time immediately puts your brain beyond its attention capacity.

$$\text{Intention} \longrightarrow \text{Attention}$$

Without *intention*, our *attention* will stray towards the content of a conversation – the topic, the job, the output of the job. It won't stay focused on how the individual is speaking or how they're behaving while they're trying to get through the content, the topic or the task in hand. It won't be focused on the kinds of behaviours I listed way back: their assertiveness, their clarity of communication, their ability to influence, their ability to organise their thinking and the thinking of others, and their ability to organise themselves.

It won't focus on any magic ingredient that makes the difference to success in the longer term. To focus on these magic ingredients, you'll need to have a stern word with yourself before you begin your observation. You'll have to set your intention. I call this a Pre-Check (you may have read about it in one of my other books). But this isn't enough; as you observe, your attention will naturally drift again – back to the task, the content, the job that's under discussion. Relax – this is normal.

Knowing that your attention will naturally drift back to the task, take regular time-outs during your observations to *push* your attention back to the individual – the person you're developing – and consciously look at their behaviours, listen to what they're saying and how they're saying it, and check how well all this is being received by others in the interaction – how effectively it's influencing, communicating, persuading, asserting, etc.

Rather than allowing a drifting focus, keep pushing your focus back to the person.

If you're involved in that interaction yourself, you might only manage three two-minute focused observations of the individual during this time, and the rest of the time your attention will quite rightly drift back to the task, the job. Don't worry – this is enough. This is plenty from which to identify behaviours, skills and thinking in the individual that you think you can help them with. It'll be challenging enough to make sure you deliberately *push* your attention back to the individual to achieve these three two-minute observations.

Chapter Nineteen

Observation three – identifying small enough chunks

> **Thinking like a developer**
>
> Cosmic Skills (too big to get your head around)
>
> Big Skills (understandable, but containing too much to work on)
>
> Small Skills (specific enough for me to get started)
>
> Behaviours, Thoughts and Things (immediately implementable)

Often, development fails because the developer isn't specific enough or because the know-how they attempt to work on is too big, i.e. the chunk of information is too big, too broad or too general.

A need such as "I want you to communicate better" is so big it's useless for our thinking or our ability to do something.

Let's call this the *Cosmic skills level* – metaphorically, it's too big to get your head around. The developer can still gain traction working at this skill level if they follow the structure of each approach fully. Each approach has features that will compensate for the target skill being "too big", as follows:

- Coach will gain traction as the learner gets specific about options they have for improving the skill.
- Sell will gain traction as the developer gets specific about "how it works".
- Teach will gain traction as the developer demonstrates the specifics they're thinking of in relation to the Cosmic skills level.
- Tell will gain traction as the developer gets specific about "the words I'd like to hear you saying" and "the movement I'd like to see you making".

But a better solution in every case is to start with a smaller chunk of information – something more specific. This requires good observation – sufficient observation to spot the possibilities available.

When you identify something like "communication" as the issue that needs development in the individual, look again. Assume there are a minimum of four chunks that make up this individual's cosmic skills level issue (four is just a mindset to help you observe – in truth, there could be 154 chunks within it, but thinking about these won't help). Let's call this next level *Big skills*. Your thinking could go like this:

Communication is this person's Cosmic skills issue. The four Big skills I think make up their communication issue are:

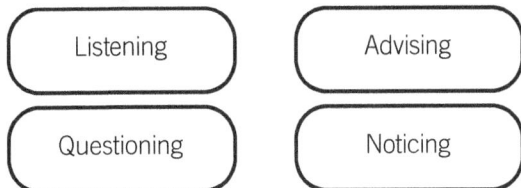

Listening	Advising
Questioning	Noticing

In another example, I could think the four Big skills that make up their communication issue are:

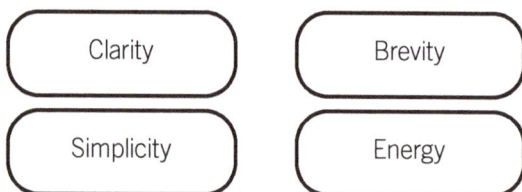

Clarity	Brevity
Simplicity	Energy

The mindset of **What if I've got it wrong?** may immediately arise at this point. But there are really only two significant problems with getting it wrong:

1 Breaking the rapport with the individual you're trying to develop (you'd have to get it horrendously wrong for this to happen).

2 Wasting time – your time and the learner's time. As I keep saying, if you're disciplined with your approach, then getting it wrong isn't a time problem – any time you waste is very small.

Sometimes a useful mindset to adopt to guard against the fear of getting it wrong is:

> Shoddy behaviour development is better than no behaviour development

Now, I'm sure this isn't always true – I'm sure there are those of us who've received such awful behaviour development that we'd have preferred none by comparison (if you're reading this and you're the recipient of just this kind of awful development, and it's been inspired by your developer reading this book, please feel free to point this paragraph out to them now). But, in the majority of cases, because most people don't receive much significant development about their behaviour or skill, there's a chance they'll just be grateful for the attention, even if your delivery isn't so good.

Back to the observation of skills and behaviours. So far we've got the following:

Cosmic skills level – too big and almost meaningless, e.g. communication.

Big skills level – a smaller chunk of information that's already more specific, e.g. listening, brevity, etc.

Once you've identified the Big skills, assume there are another four small skills that make these up, e.g. if the Cosmic skill is "communication" and the Big skill is "listening", then the Small skills might be:

Holding the silence	Summarising what's been said
Paraphrasing	Finding productive ways to interrupt

As you can see from the above, identifying this Small skills level is where your own understanding of the skill or behaviour really kicks in – this is where your observation of the individual and the context will help you identify specifics.

By the time you get to this Small skills level, you'll have a suitable-sized chunk of information to develop the learner. But you can go down a further level – this final level is Behaviours, Thoughts & Things (or BTT for short).

If you can get to this level, you can certainly deliver a short, useful, effective piece of development, e.g. if "Holding the silence" is the Small skill you decide to have a go at, then consider specific Behaviours, Thoughts or Things the individual could do or use. This will give you small chunk ideas on what you could Sell-Teach-Tell, e.g.

Behaviour

> When you're about to speak, raise your eyebrows and wait.

> Before you speak, take one deep breath in and let it out.

Thought

> If I wait, they'll run out of steam.

> In your head, say "Stop", "Wait".

Thing

> Paper and pen – when you're about to speak, write down your question.

> Carry a cup of water – when you're about to speak, take a drink instead.

Just in case it's not clear enough:

- Behaviours are what you propose they do and say – they're literally words and phrases they could use, small bodily movements or specific behaviours you suggest they do, which will take them towards the Small skill involved (in this example, "holding the silence").
- Thoughts are what you realise they could say *to themselves* – picture to themselves – which you judge will take them towards the Small skill involved.
- Things are objects or items to use somehow to develop the Small skill you're interested in. Sometimes they're objects that will distract from the wrong behaviour, e.g. taking a drink to stop yourself speaking. Sometimes they're objects that

immediately change an individual's behaviours without them having to think about anything consciously, e.g. carrying a clipboard equipped with paper and a pen can immediately induce more detailed note-taking in someone, and this can be accompanied by more focused, more attentive listening. Of course, it may produce some other behaviours that you, as the developer, don't like so much, but this is why you're going to observe again – you can help them finesse what's happening.

This may all seem a bit complicated. It really isn't – once you start observing purposefully, you can start to notice what's going on and think in this manner quickly and without much effort.

Cosmic skills

↓

Big skills   —   Small skills   —   Behaviour-Thoughts-Things

There's no right or wrong here; it's not important whether you manage to identify all levels. It doesn't matter where you choose to begin, so long as you get more specific than Cosmic skills. The only point of identifying each next-level chunk of information is to find a size of information you know you can be specific about – which you know you can describe accurately and easily, e.g. if this means you start working successfully at Big skills level, nobody cares.

Chapter Twenty

How to Sell ▶

Remember, as a development technique, Sell is about:

- Driving learning via experience.
- Driving new behaviour or skill by getting the person to try something.
- Running over the learner with a suggestion – persuading them to get on and give it a go.
- As a result, it's not detailed – it doesn't include much instruction (compared with Teach and Tell).
- It's much more about getting the learner started on something than it is about making them completely capable of delivering it.

But, remember, to Sell *you* do need to know what you want them to try – you need to be able to describe it to them.

As with coaching, there are many "selling" models available to guide you and you may already know one you prefer – so get on and use that if you're confident and comfortable. If not, here's the one we've valued most over the years. It's got a logical, easy-to-follow structure and it's straightforward.

It's based on the Persuasive Selling Format, made popular by Procter & Gamble, and each stage of its tight structure is designed to make its message more persuasive. It works like this:

1 Summarise the situation: give three to five short statements to

describe what you've noticed about the individual and what they're currently doing in the situations you've observed.

- Now nod your head or ask for their agreement – "Yes?" It's well documented that getting people to nod their head, consciously or unconsciously, makes it more likely they'll buy what you're selling – and this is no different. This is called "closing".

2   State the idea: just one short statement – the idea/approach you're selling them.

- Now close again – remember you're trying to run them over, so the more they nod and agree to what you're saying, the more likely this approach will work – "Yes?"

3   Describe how it works: use three to five short statements to explain what you think they could do.

- Close again – "Yes?"

4   Describe a couple of key benefits: things that the approach you're describing will do for them. You could ask them for a couple of benefits they think they might get as well if you like; however, the strength of the whole thing is its brevity and speed. If you give too much information, they'll start thinking too much (which really isn't the idea with this approach – action is the idea here!).

- Close again – "Yes?"

5   Close: this is the final one – you're pushing them to say they'll give your suggestion a go with phrases such as "So, are you going to do this?" and "When will you give this a try?"

This is so different from Coach. Remember, coaching is designed to generate new thinking (on the basis that they already have some of the know-how they need – they just need to *change their thinking about the situation, or about themselves, so that they can make proper use of this know-how*). Sell is not about thinking – quite the opposite. It's designed to push the individual into action – new action, new behaviour – ironically by preventing them from thinking very much and persuading them to give it a go instead.

The most difficult part of using Sell as a development technique is in keeping your statements and descriptions few in number and short in length – and in keeping your speed and energy high. If you do this, it's an effective way to create new behaviour or get someone to change existing behaviour.

To make Sell work, a number of mindset shifts suggest themselves. move your thinking as follows:

From:	Be complete	To:	Fast not perfect
From:	Make sure they know what they're doing	To:	Just get them moving – finesse it later
From:	The approach I suggest *must* work	To:	Getting them to try something different is more important than success
From:	Make sure they understand	To:	The more I say, the less likely they'll buy

With Sell, the identification of small enough chunks is essential. Your "idea" needs to be small enough for immediate implementation – tiny!

Here's a fairly obvious example. Let's say you've observed that the individual you want to develop isn't building enough rapport with the person they need to influence.

Building rapport is the Cosmic skills issue. The four Big skills you might judge make up their rapport issue are:

Listening	Matching the other person's behaviour
Communicating in a way that will appeal to the other person	Showing interest in the other person

Let's say you decide, via your observation, to work on the Big skill of "Matching the other person's behaviour". From your observation, you've noticed at least four options for the Small skills you could go for in order to develop this ability:

Noticing what the other person does and says	Using the other person's words
Using the other person's body language	Using the other person's manner – their warmth, gentleness and energy

You decide you'll try to develop the individual's ability to "Use the other person's body language". Now you break this down into some possible Behaviours, Thoughts or Things that might help.

Smile when they smile	Sit less upright (like the other person)
Use some key words the other person uses	Agree with some of the things they say

If we take the "Smile when they smile" example, this is how it might work as a Sell.

1 **Summarise the situation:**
   - "I notice you don't have the influence with this person that you'd like."
   - "You could increase your influence by giving them signals that you're more like them."
   - "In particular, I notice they smile a lot more than you – and you don't often respond."
   - "Are you with me so far? Yes?'
2 **State the idea:**
   - "So here's my idea – every time they smile, you smile back."
   - "Yes?"
3 **Describe how it works:**
   - "Here's how it works – pay attention to their face a little more."
   - "Notice when they smile – find an appropriate way to return the smile yourself."
   - "Yes? Interested?"
4 **Describe a couple of key benefits:**
   - "They'll feel you're more their kind of person."
   - "They'll place more importance on the things you say."
   - "You'll get more of the support you want from them."
5 **Close:**
   - "Want to give it go?"
   - "Good – when will you try it first?"

That's it – simple but effective.

Chapter Twenty-One

Mindset traps in Sell

Traps at "Summarise the situation":

From: I must make sure I've captured everything about the situation

and I must be complete to Fast not perfect

It's easy to be too detailed, to become too thoughtful yourself, to slow down and give too much.

Remind yourself that this is about pushing the individual into new territory and make sure your own behaviours support this. If you want them carefully thinking it through, you should Coach instead – which may take a few more minutes. Stick to three to five statements and keep them short.

"State the idea" is at risk from the same traps. Things like:

I must get it right

You don't need to get it right first time. The only reason to state the idea at all is to get a big "yes" from them. The more information you add in here, the worse it gets – one short punchy statement is enough. It doesn't even have to make much sense – all that matters is whether what you say will get a "yes". Sometimes, I make up a silly, interesting name here, rather than say anything too detailed.

Bleeding on into how it works is a danger here as well. Stop and pause once you've stated the idea. Both of you need to hear and process the "yes" from the person you're developing. Overdo the drama – wait for it. Pause. Repeat their "yes" back at them. So many managers are obsessed with creating buy-in. This is the moment, so make sure you labour it.

Traps at "Describe how it works":

Must give them the detail that's needed for them to do a good job

VS

Tiny is best

The kinds of behavioural changes people can make effectively at one time are really small – tiny, in fact. So concentrate on reducing the amount of instruction – the amount of things that you suggest – when describing how it works. Even if the person buys your suggestions, if you give them more than one or two instructions, they won't have a hope of doing them anyway.

Traps at "Describe a couple of key benefits":

These are really about how excited you're getting now. Once you start explaining why this is so good, you'll need to stop yourself. Keep it short.

Less is definitely more

Traps at "Close":

This isn't designed as a robust process, like action planning or coaching. You're just trying to make something happen. You don't want them to think about it (like you do during Coach).

So, don't drift into actions here – it's just a simple "yes" or "no" or an indication of time, e.g. "I'll start tomorrow". And, by contrast with Coach, if they say something lazy like "Immediately" here, you don't need to challenge or check this – just take it and push them on: "Go on then – go and get on." This sense of forward momentum is more important with this approach – it's what it's about after all.

If your disciplined Coach takes five minutes, then Sell should take you two to three at the most.

Chapter Twenty-Two

How to Tell

A lot of people think Sell and Tell are the same thing (and they do have their similarities in terms of their directness and how short they both are as pieces of communication). Let's explore how Tell works next, so that the critical differences between them are clear.

If we use the same example as above – working our way down from the Cosmic skill of "Building rapport" to the specific Behaviour of "Smiling when they smile" – Tell would probably work like this:

1   I'd like you to work on your rapport and influence with this person.

2   I want to *see* you smile every time they smile.

3   I don't need to *hear* anything particularly different at the moment – just concentrate on this smile.

4   I want you to create the *feeling* that you're "with them" – when they feel something deserves a smile, you do too.

Remember, Tell is designed to:

- Make new behaviours happen immediately.
- Provide such simple instructions about such small chunks of behaviour that the individual *will* be able to do them immediately.
- Help the learner to learn via experience.
- Be so direct, so assumptive about the instruction, that the learner will give the new behaviour a go (even without understanding why).

The challenges in delivering useful, powerful Tell are:

- Getting specific and simple enough about what needs to be done and said.
- Keeping your instructions clean enough – not going on and not starting to justify or give more explanation than is needed (i.e. drifting back into Sell because you feel something is missing).

To make Tell work, some mindset shifts that might be useful include moving your thinking:

From: They must know why To: *They'll* probably tell me "why" afterwards

From: I need to create buy-in first To: *They'll* buy afterwards if they like it

From: It's not right to be so direct To: If it works then it doesn't matter

From: It won't work for all kinds of reasons To: If it doesn't work, I've hardly taken any time – I can still try something else

In a development context, Tell is simple, it's targeted and, crucially, it's very specific. Remember, in order to create lasting behaviour or thinking change, the "change to make" needs to be tiny. So, Tell can work beautifully in this way:

1 You need to have done your own thinking, based on observation of the individual concerned, to identify what you think it might be helpful to change.

2 You need to have gone from Big skills through Small skills down to a Behaviour, Thought or Thing, which you'd like them to try – only this BTT level is small enough for it to stick with a Tell.

3 Give the individual a simple instruction, but make it *sensory specific*, i.e. make sure they can "picture" what it is they need to do, they can hear what it is they need to say *and* they know

the "feel" – the sense of impact you want them to aim at. This might seem tiny (and hopefully it is), but even this small amount of information could be a considerable shift for them.

Here are a few more examples for you to get the idea.

Personal organisation:
I want to see you organising your task list into three areas: quick jobs, long jobs and ongoing jobs.

Each time you identify a new task to do, I want to hear you asking yourself, "Where does this really fit?"

Create the feel of decisiveness – even if you don't have it.

Assertiveness:
I want to see you standing more upright, feet shoulder-width apart, face-on to the person you're speaking to.

I want to hear you say, "Yes, I can" or "No, I can't" and then nothing more.

I want you to create more of a feeling of "abruptness" compared with your usual communications.

Listening:
I want to see you nodding more frequently – at least a couple of times per minute.

I want to hear you repeating back key phrases the people you are listening to are using.

I want you to create the feel that you're interested and seeking more information.

Chapter Twenty-Three

Mindset traps in Tell

These are very similar to those in Coach and Sell, but more so:

They must know why | I must justify what I'm saying

You're trying to get an immediate behaviour change, so pare down your information to the tiniest possible chunks. Give it to them straight and don't extend it with whys and wherefores – they will lead you into a discussion that will take time and won't increase the likelihood the individual will try what you say. Instruct with a mindset that You're going to do this

If, once you've finished, they don't want to, then leave it there and regroup later. Moving into Coach-Sell-Teach immediately won't necessarily do the job (if you've already been very clear and this hasn't worked).

I must check they're OK

It's so easy to finish these kinds of simple instructions by accidentally continuing on into Coach because you compulsively finish with something like "How do you feel about that?" It's a nice question and a good one when establishing rapport, but it's fatal in Tell, and it's fatal to your time. Manage yourself. End the instruction and behave in a manner that communicates you expect them to get on with it.

Not my fault

Of course, this kind of development is dangerous, because if they implement your instructions and it doesn't go well for some reason (even if it's their fault) you share the responsibility for what's happened.

This doesn't mean you shouldn't Tell, but it does mean you should pay attention to this danger early. Make sure the level of change you instruct is not extreme or irresponsible. It also means you need to be a safety net. You need to remember that these were your instructions, and if they cause wider problems you'll need to explain this to others. Don't avoid this approach, but be responsible and take some responsibility afterwards – good or bad.

Need to give more and more detail, to make sure they get it right first time. Adding more information will confuse matters and, ironically, make things less clear. This one either works or it doesn't – just keep it short and straightforward, and then let them get on. If you see and hear that they haven't really understood, you can have another go. Or you can use a different approach with more understanding of what's happening, e.g. Coach if you judge they're getting in their own way somehow, in the way they're thinking about it. Or Teach if you judge they just don't have the skill to even complete your simple instruction and you actually need to show them what you mean.

Chapter Twenty-Four

Coach-Sell-Teach-Tell™ – what I notice

I notice that Coach and Tell are most frequently in use in organisational life.

Coach often turns up as crap coaching, where you already know what you want me to think, say and do, but you do this bizarre bit of judo questioning to try to get me to say it. Time-consuming, pointless, dishonest and very frustrating.

Tell often turns up as one big bit of bossiness or opinion, where you tell me in no uncertain terms what you think I should do – but you don't break it down for me into a tiny, tiny chunk of sensory-specific information (see-hear-feel), which I can actually follow. So the usual Tell that lurks around our workplaces is difficult to do anything with and often in danger of making me feel stupid.

Sell turns up as a big and detailed discussion or debate, in which you try to reason things through with me and get me to do something you want via this reasoning through. As a result, I often resist. And when I do, rather than back off, you keep going and going – on and on, trying to find different reasons why I should do what you're suggesting. Very time-consuming, and exhausting for us both, with no real breakthrough resulting.

Teach. In truth, I don't see Teach much at all. Even as I write this, I'm doing a long search through my memory of learning during my nine years in organisational life. During those nine years, I was lucky enough to receive one very well-structured experience receiving Teach, and this was during a six-week off-job training to do a very particular task. This piece of development concentrated on teaching me both process and behaviours – which itself was a unique approach in the development I received. But I notice that, while it was rigorous in its Teach structure and approach with regards to the process it was teaching (a button-pushing, form-filling, way-of-thinking kind of process), as soon as it switched into helping me with my behaviours (what I needed to be like while pushing the buttons, and in response to other people who would challenge me to push the buttons differently), essential elements of Teach were fudged or just disappeared altogether. This is really typical of what we see: if Teach gets done methodically, it usually crops up in the early stages of helping you cope with button-pushing and form-filling (although, even here, it's often fudged).

This doesn't mean my six weeks' training wasn't any good – it was an excellent and illuminating experience, and prepared me brilliantly for the following year of my career. But, where behaviours were concerned, with just a few small adjustments it could have been even better – quicker and more effective in producing behavioural change in me.

By contrast, outside of organisational life, the twenty days of NLP Practitioner training and then the 20 days of NLP Master Practitioner training I invested in with an independent supplier, were immaculately structured to follow the Teach cycle – and, boy, was this effective in changing my behaviours at the same time as getting me proficient in multiple processes and ways of working.

Chapter Twenty-Five

How to Teach

Remember, as a development technique, Teach is designed to:

- Give clarity about what to do and how to do it.
- Perform powerful neurosurgery – getting the learner's brain ready to do the new behaviour (or process).
- Allow practice – the opportunity to experience the new behaviour, now, for yourself.
- Get the learner feeling more comfortable with the new behaviour.
- Help you to "walk things through for yourself" (compared with Coach's intention to get you to "think things through for yourself".
- Start to push new behaviour *into the part of your brain where it needs to live* if you're going to do it in practical situations, after the development session has ended.

Our simple model for Teach is EDIC. Not sure where this originated, but it is probably a military instructional tool.

E is for Explain:

"This is what you do; this is why you do it."

It's about clarity – preparing you to look out for what's important in the new behaviour that you're about to see and hear.

D is for Demonstrate:

"Let me show you what I mean – here's how to do it."

I, as the developer, actually do what I'm talking about. Don't jump to the conclusion that this is a role-play (it could be, but it's not always relevant or the best approach). Remember, you're showing such tiny chunks of behaviour that you might not need an interaction provided by a role-play. You might achieve a better transfer of behaviour without. And, as usual, you don't want to spend much time, so anything you do that increases the time taken isn't necessarily a good thing to do.

I is for Implement or Imitate:
"Go on then – show me."

The developer gets the learner to have a go themselves.

C is for Consolidate:
The developer, observing what the learner is doing during the Imitate stage, provides quick feedback and suggestions to get the learner to have another go, amending their approach somehow. Essentially, you play with and tinker about with what you're seeing and hearing the learner do – working to make it look, sound and feel more like you think it should. During this process, the learner's brain continues to assimilate the behaviour – making it their own, making it "authentic", pushing it towards a repeatable-on-command skill.

Here's a simple example, considering it might have a military application:

> Sergeant Major (stood in front of the Private): "When carrying your gun, point it at the floor at all times, and keep the safety on. If it goes off by accident, you won't kill me − if you're lucky, you'll only shoot yourself in the foot."
> "Let me show you…"
> Sergeant Major walks up and down with the gun pointed at the floor.

"Right – show me."

Sergeant Major hands the gun to Private.

"STTOPPPPP!"

Private pauses.

"AT THE FLOOR, I SAID...AT THE FLOOR!"

Private changes stance.

"Yes, that's better."

Red in the face, Sergeant Major takes the gun back.

"Now – have another go."

Hands the gun to Private.

Each of these steps has an important neurological function and each step, as it's added, makes it more likely, neurologically, that the new behaviour will stick and become a repeatable behaviour (a skill).

Explain: Here, you're priming the learner's brain. You're getting it ready to pay attention to the important points of the demonstration you're about to perform. Don't give too much information here – target the crucial points. Don't overload your learner's attention system. The more you add in, the more likely they'll pay particular attention to the wrong parts of your demonstration.

Demonstrate: it's strongly suspected that (like the brains of other apes) human brains contain cells called mirror neurons. When your senses observe other humans doing things, these are brain cells that literally mirror – they begin to replicate these behaviours. Neurologically, to do this, they stimulate the formation of new networks of brain cells – wiring connections across the brain that will be needed in order for the observer to do the self-same action. Essentially, this means that when you observe a behaviour you haven't seen before, you immediately start to complete that behaviour yourself – in your brain – constructing the hardware and software required to replicate it. When children watch a famous footballer on TV doing a new move, a new twist or turn with the ball, their brains imitate the move – their brains get capable and ready for them to do it themselves in the playground the next day.

Implement or Imitate: Crucially, though our brains now have the hardware and software available to perform the new behaviour, nevertheless the wiring isn't strong – it isn't well- formed as yet. To strengthen the connections in the learner's brain, the learner needs to do the behaviours for themselves.

But since the behaviour is so new, the thinking brain (the prefrontal cortex) – that bit of your brain just behind your forehead – seizes control of the performance of the new behaviour. This allows you to be highly conscious of what you're doing – literally, you're thinking your way through the new behaviour. This is positive and necessary – it's your brain paying acute attention to what's going on. It's your conscious mind working as hard as it can to "get it right".

But if, by the end of the development, the new behaviour is still controlled by the prefrontal cortex, then it's at risk of not being used. This is because any time you try it you'll "think your way through it". As a result, it's going to feel particularly clunky, unnatural and not comfortable. Repetition is essential to move the behaviour from the prefrontal cortex to the basal ganglia (the habit centre in the mid-brain). In truth, the new behaviour is unlikely to feel "comfortable" until the learner has done enough repetition.

As developers, we need to pay great attention to this. Learners we're working with will quickly report their discomfort with new behaviour, but they'll use it as an objection to learning. As soon as you ask them to try something different, they'll say things like:
"It feels clunky."
"It doesn't feel authentic."
"It doesn't feel natural."
"It doesn't feel like me."

Well, of course – they're correct. It doesn't. The challenge is that learners will regularly use this feeling as proof that the new behaviour is wrong, is not for them, is not to be practised. This is understandable but faulty thinking, and it's your responsibility as the developer to push them to stick with the necessary steps, so that they can move beyond clunky, inauthentic, not natural, not me. Only once they've done this can they really judge whether this behaviour feels like something they can use themselves – authentically.

This is a crucial intention of Implement or Imitate. But, to make it work effectively, this step needs to interact meaningfully with the next – Consolidate.

Consolidate: One of the problems with role-play is that we put all the time into getting the right behaviour out of the learner. We get lost in the role-play itself and finally stop it *at the point where the learner gets it right*. "Correct – that's it – well done." Neurologically, this is a seriously faulty approach to learning. We know that repetition of new behaviour is needed in order to move the behaviour from the prefrontal cortex to the habit centre (the basal ganglia). But it's essential that the behaviour we get the learner to repeat is "*the correct*" *behaviour*.

This is what Consolidate is all about. So, for Teach to work effectively, we need to give feedback as early and as quickly as possible – do what's needed to move the learner to the "correct" version of the new behaviour immediately. Once this is achieved, you can use the time available to get them to *repeat the correct behaviour* a number of times.

"Great – show me again."
"That's it – and again."
"Perfect – one more time."
"And one more."

Chapter Twenty-Six

Mindset traps in Teach

Mindset traps during Explain:

Many of the same mindsets we've considered before will crop up when starting to explain:

From:	They must know why	To:	They'll probably tell me "why" afterwards
From:	I need to create buy-in first	To:	They'll buy afterwards if they like it
From:	It's not right to be so direct	To:	If it works then it doesn't matter
From:	It won't work for all kinds of reasons	To:	If it doesn't work, I've hardly taken any time – I can still try something else

Of course, all the pink highlighted thoughts above are valid and appropriate. A small slice of them will be helpful. But, as I've said too many times already, where development is concerned less is more – less is more likely to actually turn into a change of approach or behaviour. So, if the choice is between talking through "why" and "what for" or getting on and demonstrating the new behaviour, I'd recommend you go for the demonstration every time.

The biggest trap with Explain is that it's easy to do. The learner will be happy to listen to you. So, frequently, what happens is that the developer explains, and then they explain some more, and more and more. In fact, often, as a developer, it's too easy to think you've completed a full EDIC Teach cycle when all you've done is a very, very long Explain (which misses the point of the whole thing). This happens on a regular basis during training courses: Explain as a substitute for Teach. The trainer never steps up and shows you how to do the thing they're teaching you. They never get you to have a go yourself. Instead, much training remains stuck in the ill-conceived 1970s method – question and answer, followed by a discussion, followed by a clarification at the flipchart, often writing down in front of the audience the conclusions of the discussion. No demonstration of what you actually do with the information. No requirement that the learner actually does something immediately with the information (unless it's a lame role-play). No repetition of the new behaviour. As I've said, when we use a lame role-play, it usually stops once we've got the point – it doesn't get repeated, doing the correct behaviour over and over.

So, the first challenge with Teach is to shorten the explanation and get to the important stuff.

Mindset traps during Demonstrate:

A key trap here is the thought that:

I must know how to do this thing myself   or   I must get everything correct in my demonstration

Actually, it's better to move into the demonstration phase with a mindset of:

Let's just give it a go   and   We can play with this 'til it's right

If you've got rapport with the person you're helping to develop, then you won't need to know exactly how to do the thing you want to Teach them.

Just enough to get going You only need to know enough to give it a first try – you don't need to be good yourself during your first demonstration. All that's needed is that you show them the kind of thing you think they should be doing – a rough approximation. This will be enough to start the process of change in the learner's brain. Once you've done this, you can let them show you (Implement or Imitate), and you can watch and play with what they do (Consolidate) until they, themselves, get it to the level of proficiency you think is needed. If this is how you work, then a mindset of **I'm learning as much as you** will be important (it's not only a mindset – it's possibly the truth as well).

At Implement and Consolidate, at least two traps can present themselves:

1. **What about this?** and **What about that?** When you ask the person you're working with to have a go at the behaviour themselves – "Go on – show me" – they may feel foolish, embarrassed, shy, scared. It's normal for them to respond by asking for information or questioning the purpose, the significance, etc. Be mindful of this response – often they're just trying to avoid the discomfort of doing the new behaviour themselves. In response to this, you should make sure you maintain your connection with them, e.g. acknowledge their questions, smile, even answer one of them. But then you'll need to push and insist they give it a try.

2. **I'm embarrassed – this is patronising** If there's a moment when Teach feels patronising, this is it! Asking the person to show you the behaviour again and again doesn't feel "right" somehow. This is really why I've been highlighting the significance of the neurology; you need to hold your confidence

that the repetition, while it may feel patronising, is the essential "gift" that will make the difference to the individual's ability to develop. Not only this, of course – it's the repetition that allows the individual to play with the new behaviour and do it in their own way (this increases the likelihood that you can get through the objection that "this doesn't feel authentic").

Finally, remember the key principle in using Teach is to make sure that you allow the individual to perform the new behaviour correctly and *then* begin the process of repetition.

Chapter Twenty-Seven

Rapport and connection

Well, that's it in terms of the specifics of how to do each approach.

Before we finish, though, I want to go back to the central issues. Because, while it's vital you learn and stick with the discipline of the simple structure of each approach, the things that will make the difference to your effective use of these simple structures are once again:

- Your intention to develop the individual – this by itself will take you a long way.
- Your observation – vital to give you context, help you pinpoint what you might help with, identify the capability levels already present and decide the approach you might take.
- Your connection with the individual concerned – your rapport, the key thing that will decide whether they're interested in whatever you do with them.

The most significant of these is connection or rapport. It's worth saying again just how important this is. It won't matter whether you do any of the four approaches particularly brilliantly; if you don't have rapport – a good connection with the individual you're working with – it's likely that your brilliant approach won't make a difference. It's possible they won't even find it relevant.

Recently, I was discussing the concepts of this book with a manager attending some development I was delivering. She raised a couple of important objections to the idea of short development sessions – sessions using the timescales I listed before (i.e. Coach – five minutes, Sell – three minutes, Teach – ten minutes, Tell – one minute).

Her concerns were:

1   Accidentally communicating rudeness to the person you're developing – rudeness caused by breaking off a session because you're "keeping it deliberately short" (e.g. at the coffee machine), or because you realise the approach you're using isn't working and you should back off and park it for another time.

2   Accidentally communicating that you don't value what the individual is saying – "First you invite them to open up and talk to you (e.g. if you're coaching), then you tell them time's up – effectively you close down the thinking you've invited them to open up."

Both are important and useful objections to keep in mind. Rudeness and undervaluing people are certainly not going to help you develop them.

Just to re-emphasise, though, this rudeness and undervaluing won't be produced simply by the shortness of the development sessions you provide – rudeness and undervaluing are not *always* time-dependent. Usually, again, they're about your manner and about the behaviours you use to communicate things like time constraints. You can be brief without communicating that you're rushing a conversation.

Neither of these objections (rudeness or undervaluing) should stop you taking the approaches described in this book. Neither is about the efficient and time-bound use of Coach-Sell-Teach-Tell™. Both are really about the quality of rapport you've established with the individual you're developing. This rapport needs to be good regardless of the approach you're taking. It's this rapport – or lack of it – that will determine whether they receive your brief interaction as highly productive or somewhat offensive.

If you make sure you establish a good rapport with those you're developing, they'll forgive you when you get it wrong – when you challenge too hard, when you push too far.

If you're connected with the individual, they will know you "get them" on some level, even though you may not agree with what they say. If you're connected with the individual, they will even forgive you if you accidentally communicate "haste" when you merely meant to keep things brief and simple. If you're connected with the individual, they will forgive you if you suddenly need to call a halt to a session because you have to get to a meeting or something else demands your attention.

- So, if you too are worried about being rude or undervaluing people, take another look at chapter 12 on connection. Or, better still, find a book dedicated to rapport or listening – there are many available. Rapport is the key skill that empowers whatever approach you take. And strong listening is the key skill in rapport.

Remember, the timings I've proposed are mindsets only – they're your intention, rather than what you actually do. I'm proposing that if you listen well, and you stop interjecting with your own thinking, on many occasions you'll find that five minutes of Coaching is actually a lot of quality thinking time – as much as is needed by the individual concerned.

This doesn't mean you shouldn't ever go beyond these timings. You need to judge when a piece of development may need to take longer. My key point throughout this book has been to make sure that it *is* a *judgement* – not an autopilot wander into overly long development sessions.

My objective with this book has been to get you to provide *more* development. I've only been encouraging you to think it takes little time in order that you provide more and do it more frequently. If you want to take longer – if you believe you *should* take longer, so as not to be rude or undervalue the person you're working with, this is, of course, not a problem.

Yesterday, I spent a whole day with one field manager, developing them in the behaviours, thinking and processes of good field management. A whole day! In truth, there were six or seven hour-long chunks to the day, and each hour-long chunk was made up of the kind of mad mix of Coach-Sell-Teach-Tell™, which, back at the beginning, I described my guitar teacher using. Being a developer is my full-time job, so I'm frequently developing people for an hour or more at a time. The important point about the time issue is your ability to choose. Yesterday, once or twice, I may even have Coached for as much as thirty minutes before switching to Teach or Tell. But I knew I was doing this. And I already have the ability, the discipline, the skill and the intention needed to deliver five-minute sessions whenever I want to as well – whenever I judge this is required. So, I rarely surrender to my autopilot (I say rarely – nobody's perfect!).

Take as long as you like with the development you provide – but *not* if this stops you developing people regularly and *not* because you're lazy and ill-disciplined, not because your rapport skills are not good enough to mean you won't upset people with short sessions, and not because you've failed to develop enough rapport with the individual to get away with brief interactions without them thinking you're rude.

Chapter Twenty-Eight

In summary

I could go on, adding more and more layers of skill, significance and meaning. I could add more systematic ways of assessing the blocks in people, listening for different blocks, responding to these different blocks with different methods of moving their thinking from one place to another, specific ways of overcoming their objections, processes targeted to change their mindsets and so on. But, as you know by now, that's not the intention of this book. I need to hold my own discipline in the same way I've been advocating – not get too interested; not start indulging my own knowledge; not carrying on just because there *is* more; not start showing off.

I'm hoping that, by this point, while we might have covered quite a number of concepts, there are still a small enough number of principles for you to get on immediately and begin to practise something following your first reading.

So, finally, to help pull your thinking together, I'll summarise the key points of the Coach–Sell–Teach–Tell™ approach one last time, and in one place. After that, we're done, and it's time for you to get out there and have a go.

Coach-Sell-Teach-Tell™ – the approach

1   Have an intention to develop skills in your people – get beyond the task stuff.

2   Observe them. Start to think about them as a person and consider what the magic ingredient is that's stopping them from completing pieces of work effectively. Think about the behaviour or skill that's critically missing, rather than the head knowledge required to do the task.

3   Don't observe for long. Aim for several two-minute conscious observations and draw your conclusions enough to get going on their development.

4   Connect. Once you're clear enough on a behaviour or skill you want to start with, make sure you've put enough effort and energy into getting a good connection – enough rapport:
    - Get them talking and show your interest.
    - Pay attention to what they say – repeat key points back and acknowledge what's important.
    - Ask about the areas you're thinking of developing them in. Check whether they're interested yet – whether they think they're already skilled in these areas. Demonstrate your interest in their responses. Listen properly. Show you're listening.

5   Don't let yourself believe that establishing rapport will take long – it's quick with focused attention.

6   Observe again – a number of times. Know that your attention will automatically drift to the task, the content of the discussion or the meeting. You'll have to consciously move it back to their behaviour – how they do and say things, how they organise themselves, etc.

7   Continue to observe and consider whether they have enough existing skills already (in this situation, in another situation or just generally in life) and therefore whether you can Coach them.

8   If the answer is "no", consider how much time you have available and how much know-how you have yourself about the behaviour you want to develop.

9   If you're not Coaching, pick from Sell, Teach or Tell, depending on whether you want to:

a) Just get them moving and trying things – Sell or Teach

b) Be precise about what you're after – Tell

c) Actually improve their skill and ability to implement it immediately – Teach

10   With Sell, Teach or Tell, identify small things to work on – tiny things! Move your thinking from Cosmic skills to Big skills to Small skills to Behaviours, Thoughts and Things.

11   Remember the mindset of how much time could be enough:

- Five minutes: Coach

- Three minutes: Sell

- Ten minutes: Teach

- One minute: Tell

Of course, these timescales are only guidelines to make sure you know you can achieve meaningful development in short amounts of time; they're not a requirement. Longer Coaching sessions will be great – not necessarily better – but people will enjoy the attention.

12   Vary your approach – don't get stuck in a rut. Stimulate and maintain the interest of those you're helping to develop. This will keep both of you engaged and learning.

13   Let go of your notions that one approach may be better than another – they each have their features and benefits. They're just different and they do different jobs, and require different things from you.

14   Keep it simple. Stick with the simplicity of each structure so that you're able to learn it, repeat it and free your attention for listening and maintaining your connection with people.

15   Know the structures work and that you don't need to add in more clever techniques or approaches.

16   Keep observing the people you're developing so that you can see, hear and feel what might be required next, and what might be the best approach for dealing with this.

17   Pay attention to the blocks they might put up – the objections or barriers. These will instruct you what to do next, e.g. you

might need to Coach to get them thinking differently in order to overcome the block that's now presenting (as a result of the development you've done so far), or you might need to respond to a block with a simple Tell – a more direct instruction to get on with it. *Who knows?! So keep thinking and keep observing – this is a dynamic and ongoing process.*

18   Pay attention to their responses – keep listening. When you notice that you've overstepped the mark – you've pushed too hard or been too insistent about an approach to take – back off and put more time into re-establishing your connection (remember that listening is key to this).

19   Don't let yourself assume that rebuilding rapport is a big job – it shouldn't take long if you put focused attention into it.

20   Provide lots of short development sessions over the long term.

Make a difference to each person – actually develop them!

See their behaviours and their thinking change, and see their skills develop.

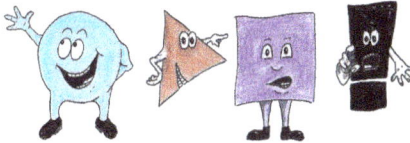

Acknowledgements

As this book goes to print, it's been 20 years since Doug and I began the venture that would become Coloured Square Limited – a venture which would produce so much simple, powerful clarity for people – a toolkit for communication, management, leadership, credibility and learning which so many people have enjoyed and valued during these years.

Whilst Doug hasn't actually taken an active part in the writing process for this book, its contents are 100% an output of our many discussions, debates and learning together. A big thanks to him for being such an amazing business partner, learner, friend and foil for so many years.

We've been playing with the GROW cycle in our own coaching practise for many years. One of my earliest investigations of it was in reading Sir John Whitmore's brilliant *Coaching for Performance*. Whilst we haven't been able to identify a single 'owner' of the GROW cycle, clearly its popularity and continued usage across many years is heavily indebted to the work of Graham Alexander, Alan Fine and Sir John Whitmore, together with other influential work by Max Landsberg and by Timothy Gallwey whose own work influenced those listed above. Whilst they're not directly referenced in the pages describing Coach, we have read and thought about their work, amongst many other coaching practitioners, such as Robert Dilts and Ian McDermott over the years. We haven't re-read any of them for some time now, but it's appropriate to acknowledge their inevitable contribution to the thinking that has finally resulted in this book.

Similarly, we've tried to find the origins of the EDIC cycle without success, and we cannot remember where we first came across it. Suffice it to say that, whoever they are, we're grateful they kicked off our thinking by coming up with this powerful framework, though we may have changed the context and the detail of its usage somewhat.

Finally, as I've listed a couple of times in the main text already, we're indebted to P&G for their promotion of the Persuasive Selling Format (PSF) for use by their sales teams. Whilst we've changed the context entirely here, and somewhat changed the sense of the model, Doug received the best and most valuable training of his life from P&G, and this is one of many principles and ways of working that have remained with him in very practical ways ever since.

Big thanks too to Alison Rogers, Andrew Manuel and Luke Thomas for being such a great team and continuing to take part so actively in our ongoing learning.

And to John Nixon, whose continued wisdom over the years has been a source of strength and confidence.

Many other people have contributed over the years in some way to the ideas that have resulted in this book. And I'd like to thank a few of them for their part in the debates that have led to the final clarity of the idea I've been describing. In no particular order, I'd include Pauline Bennett, Susan Brodie, Jennie Davis, Sarah Henson, James Iles, Roger Minton, Lorna Tolley-Poulson, Mel Pyke, and Jill Youds – you may not know it, but you've played a part in this somewhere.

Thanks to Penny Richardson for continuing to be such an unsung, practical support in the running of our business.

And finally, thanks to my wife Jo, and my children, Emma, Jacob, Harriet and Jacob who continue to support and indulge me in my various creative flights of fancy.